The Business Value of DB2 for z/OS

IBM DB2 Analytics Accelerator and Optimizer

John Campbell
Namik Hrle
Ruiping Li
Surekha Parekh
Terry Purcell

MC PRESS

MC Press Online, LLC
Boise, ID 83703

The Business Value of DB2 for z/OS:
IBM DB2 Analytics Accelerator and Optimizer
John Campbell, Ruiping Li, Surekha Parekh, and Terry Purcell

First Edition
First Printing—March 2013
Second Printing—May 2013

MC Press offers excellent discounts on this book when ordered in quantity for bulk purchases or special sales.

MC Press Online, LLC, 3695 W. Quail Heights Court, Boise, ID 83703-3861 USA
Customer Service: (208) 629-7275 ext. 500; service@mcpressonline.com
Permissions and Special Orders: mcbooks@mcpressonline.com
On the Web: www.mc-store.com

ISBN: 978-1-58347-381-8

About the Authors

John Campbell (campbelj@uk.ibm.com) is an IBM®
Distinguished Engineer reporting to the Director for
z/OS® Development at the IBM Silicon Valley Lab. He has
extensive experience of DB2® in terms of systems, database,
and applications design. John specializes in design for high
performance and data sharing. He is one of IBM's foremost
authorities for implementing high-end database/transaction-
processing applications.

Namik Hrle works in the IBM Boeblingen Development Laboratory and is the lab's chief Information Management technologist,
responsible for strategy and technology directions. As an IBM
Distinguished Engineer and a member of the IBM Academy
of Technology, he belongs to a small circle of the top technical
leaders whose work and expertise affect the direction of IBM.
He is a member of the Information Management Architecture
Board, Software Group Architecture Board Steering Committee,
Technical Experts Council, and many other IBM expert teams that
work on strategic technology topics as well as address customers' information technology needs and requirements. He is the holder of numerous patents, outstanding technical
achievements, and author recognition and corporate awards.

Ruiping Li is a Senior Engineer in DB2 for z/OS development at
IBM Silicon Valley Lab. She is the technical lead responsible for
the DB2 query acceleration support for the IBM DB2 Analytics
Accelerator. She has been the development lead for DB2 9 for z/
OS new feature optimistic locking support and DB2 10 for z/OS
new feature timestamp with time zone data type support and has
also been the key developer for some other important functionality. This functionality includes pureXML index exploitation,
complex queries, MQTs, and multiple CCSID features in DB2
for z/OS.

Surekha Parekh (surekhaparekh@uk.ibm.com) is IBM's World-Wide Marketing Program Director for DB2 for z/OS and also leads the Social Media Strategy for Information Management on System z. She is responsible for market strategy and planning of DB2 on System z® and building social media communities for Information Management System z. Based in Warwick, United Kingdom, Surekha is a passionate marketer with proven results. She has over 25 years of business experience, and she is also passionate about Information Management. Surekha represents IBM on the IDUG committee. IDUG is an independent DB2 user group with more than 16,000 members in more than 100 countries.

Terry Purcell (tpurcel@us.ibm.com) is a Senior Technical Staff Member with the IBM Silicon Valley Lab, where he is lead designer for the DB2 for z/OS Optimizer. Terry has two decades of experience with DB2 in database administration and application development as a customer, consultant, and DB2 developer.

Contents

Foreword

Parents never know how their children will turn out. But if they turn out well, then we take credit for it. DB2 for z/OS, which will be 30 years old in 2013, has turned out well, and though I'd like to think it was all because of the parents, the facts are different. First let me assert that DB2 for z/OS is heavily used by enterprises worldwide to perform database functions for core business transactions and analytics—others can provide the statistics to back this assertion. The question is why this is so for a 30-year-old technology, when a few years is a lifetime in our business. I attribute it to six critical factors:

1. **Great foundation:** IBM Research pioneered the relational data model, and the System R project provided the core technology for DB2 for z/OS. The partnership between research and development was solidified with the development of the Data Base Technology Institute (DBTI) led by Pat Selinger, which linked up research and development personnel to solve tough technology problems.

2. **Customers:** DB2's success depends on its customers' success. In the 1970s, databases served a single application. Because hardware was so expensive and slow, the database had to be handcrafted for each application. But this led to a proliferation of data, giving rise to the notion of "data independence," which allowed a database to be shared by many applications. The key notion was **anticipating the unanticipated**. The challenge was making the technology perform well and at acceptable costs. DB2 partnered with customers to drive this notion for 30 years.

3. **Integration with the Z-ecosystem:** DB2 lives within the Z environment and is critically dependent on it for hardware, application development tools, transaction management, storage management, system management, network management, business intelligence tools, and so much more. Integration with all of the parts of that ecosystem and leveraging its capabilities provides a compelling, holistic service.

4. **Partnership with practitioners and partners:** Customer executives buy DB2, but database administrators make it work. The journey of DB2 has been a close partnership with practitioners led by customer advisory councils, the International DB2 Users Group (IDUG), SHARE/GUIDE, and close personal relationships.

5. **Evolving DB2 as the world changes:** The mainframe has evolved into a multi-core Sysplex, and DB2 evolved its architecture to support a data sharing environment. DB2 has evolved with distributed database processing, the Internet, SOA, Java, Big Data, and every change that the industry has made. The recent delivery of the zEC12 DB2 Analytics Accelerator, which is a joint effort between System Z, DB2, and Netezza® to serve Big Data with near-real time analysis, continues this leadership in innovation.

6. **Technologists:** DB2 has been blessed with great innovators. Namik Hrle and Guogen Zhang, who led the innovation of the Analytics Accelerator, join a long list of talented technologists who have made DB2 respond to the next challenge and delight customers.

Happy Birthday!

Don Haderle—Father of DB2

Introduction

We hope you enjoy our new book. This book has been launched to celebrate the 30th anniversary of DB2. Many of you will remember that the first release of DB2 was launched on June 7, 1983—marking the birth of relational database. At the time of launch, there were many skeptics about the relational database. Thirty years later, the relational database market continues to grow stronger and stronger, and according to analysts at IDC, it is expected reach over $41 billion by 2016 (source: "RDBMS Steamrolls into 2016 on BI, Big Data Expectations," *Information Management*, August 20, 2012; *http://www.information-management.com/news/rdbms-steamrolls-into-2016-on-bi-big-data-expectations-10023040-1.html*).

The book is divided into three sections. The first section celebrates our anniversary and thanks our customers, business partners, and users for their commitment and loyalty. It begins with a special message from the "Father of DB2"—Donald Haderle. Then DB2 customers, Business Partners, and IBMers discuss important milestones, share memories, tell us what makes DB2 so great, and let us know why they think DB2 is still around and growing three decades later. Finally, IBM's leaders share their thoughts about the strengths and future of DB2.

The next section begins with a technical DB2 Analytics Accelerator white paper that covers the key design and operational aspects that enable DB2 for IBM z/OS clients to benefit from faster performance, reduced CPU usage, and lower costs.

The heart of the book is packed with business value, such as performance enhancements and cost-saving measures, and is full of rich hints and tips. The objective is to help our customers to upgrade to the latest version of DB2 so that they can start reaping the performance and CPU savings that many of our early adopters are experiencing. An excellent paper by Terry Purcell, an IBM expert, discusses query performance and DB2 Optimizer. Terry understands the key customer pains, such as "reducing total cost of ownership" while maintaining stability and reliability, and his paper discusses how DB2 10 addresses these issues. Next, John Campbell, IBM Distinguished Engineer, has updated his DB2 10 for z/OS upgrade planning paper, adding experiences and lessons learnt that have been gained from customers and covering key secrets to ensure a successful upgrade.

The final section presents a collection of DB2 customer case studies in which customers share their migration experiences and articulate the business benefits they are seeing since upgrading to our latest release.

I would like to thank Don Haderle, John Campbell, Terry Purcell, and Ruiping Li and her coauthors for their contributions to this fantastic book. Without these experts, there would not be a book.

We would also like to thank all our customers, partners, IBMers, and the extended DB2 community for your continued support and loyalty. We invite you to join our virtual communities (see URLs below) so that you can keep in touch with our DB2 experts, developers, and extended IBM community. These communities are available 24x7 with over 7,000 members. They are a great way to meet like-minded individuals, have fun, and at the same time grow and develop your skills.

Throughout 2013, IBM will be hosting several DB2 seminars, conferences, and events around the world to celebrate DB2's 30th anniversary with our fans. Information about these events will be shared via the 30th Anniversary Facebook Fan Page, *http:// www.facebook.com/IBMDB2forzOS.*

I hope you enjoy the book. Please do not hesitate to contact me directly if I can be of help to you in any way.

Surekha Parekh
World-Wide Marketing Program Director
IBM DB2 for z/OS
February 2013

Useful URLs

The World of DB2 for z/OS
http://db2forzos.ning.com

IBM Website
http://www-01.ibm.com/software/data/db2/zos/family

DB2 10 for z/OS
http://www.ibm.com/software/data/db2/db210

YouTube
http://www.youtube.com/user/IBMDB2forzOS

Surekha Parekh's DB2 Blog
http://surekhaparekh.wordpress.com

LinkedIn Group
http://www.linkedin.com/groups?gid=2821100

Twitter
http://twitter.com/IBMDB2

International DB2 Community
http://www.idug.org

30 Years of Innovation

DB2 customers discuss important milestones, what makes DB2 so great, and why DB2 is still around today

Manuel Gómez Burriel,
Spanish Confederation of Savings Banks (CECA)

DB2 Version 3 partition independence for utilities changed the way and strategy for how historical information was managed . . . and it is still working right today. I also remember Roger Miller speaking at SpDUG in 2010 . . . it was a milestone for the Spanish community.

DB2 is the most appropriate relational database management system (RDBMS) for the z/OS platform, capable of running any data management application—whether transactional or data warehousing or whatever. Because of the evolution of new versions and new appliance add-ons, DB2 has had, and will continue to have, a long journey in the IT world.

About Manuel Gómez Burriel

Manuel Gómez Burriel is DBA Manager at the Spanish Confederation of Savings Banks (CECA). Being involved in DBA tasks for more than 26 years, he has had to face different DBMS flavors: IMS™, DB2, and others. IMS was Manuel's first approach to a DBMS, and it has accompanied him for his whole working life with total loyalty and fidelity. "We recently celebrated our silver wedding," says Manuel. "But then, DB2 arrived with new ideas, concepts, and attractive enhancements and functionalities. Now we were a triangle. . .and, as many of you know, triangles are not good in the relationship fields. But we were able to coexist, taking advantage of the best of everyone; and we have lived happily ever after."

Frank Petersen, JN Data A/S

In the history of DB2, I would like to draw two things forward: First, around 1987, Provinsbanken in Denmark announced that they moved their core banking system to DB2. The whole world watched and went to huge presentations at the Provinsbanken site to see with their own eyes. Suddenly, the community could see that DB2 meant serious business, and the reputation of "too slow" and "too unreliable" disappeared almost overnight. The second thing was the arrival of DB2 data sharing in Version 4 around 1995. This masterpiece of design set the cornerstone of the scalability in DB2 that has made it possible to get to the point where we are now.

Why is DB2 great and still around? In my opinion, there are two important aspects: First, DB2 has always had a very lively and enthusiastic user community. Many users consider DB2 as more than "just work" and are delivering a huge voluntary effort to improve the product and its usage across all installations. Second, IBM has been very clever in delivering the right functionality at the right time. We know all the major disciplines: performance, reliability, and scalability. And we sort of take them for granted. However, as users we must understand that the product we get today was designed three to four years ago, so it is very important that the designers have a very good feeling for what the market will need three to five years forward from a given point. This understanding of the market comes partly as a result of IBM's huge involvement in the community, but also the other way 'round: as a result of the user community's huge involvement in the DB2 evolution. So, in my opinion, it is a sort of yin and yang between the community and IBM that has made the difference.

About Frank Petersen

Frank Petersen has worked as a systems programmer in large installations since 1978 and has been involved in every DB2 release since Version 1, working with the technical side of almost every aspect of DB2. Besides DB2 on z/OS, Frank has worked with DB2 LUW and also has a broad insight into "modern" things like Web development, .Net, Java, and more. Frank has been a speaker at many events organized by IBM, GSE, and IDUG. He has received IDUG's Best Speaker Award numerous times and therefore is a member of IDUG's Speaker Hall of Fame.

Jan Tielemans, KBC Global Services NV

The most remarkable DB2 milestone for me was the introduction of DB2 data sharing!

What makes DB2 so great, and the reason it is still around today, is its nearly "unlimited" possibilities. DB2 keeps growing in function and features according to the market/customer needs. . .and the great technical support and user group community that exist around this great product.

About Jan Tielemans

Jan Tielemans has worked with DB2 since V1.2, as a DB2 system engineer and as a senior technical specialist for DB2 products for many years at Platinum Technology and BMC Software. He is currently employed at KBC Global Services, working as a senior system engineer on the DB2 team. Jan's areas of expertise include DB2 performance and tuning, data sharing, and Parallel Sysplex. Jan's current position is Mainframe Resource Manager. He is also chairman of the Belgium IMS/DB2 GSE workgroup.

Dave Beulke, Dave Beulke & Associates

I have worked with DB2 since Version 1.2 for z/OS and with DB2 LUW since it was OS/2 Extended Edition. Working with the DB2 family over the years has been great because of the performance, integrity, and scalability of the database and the quality of the IBM developers and management behind it.

I remember being in the beta program for the first DB2 data sharing release, DB2 Version 4 for z/OS. I realized then that working with DB2's unlimited scalability, there are no limits to the business solutions that can be built, and the only limitation was my imagination. DB2 continues to lead the database management system (DBMS) industry because it embraces change and expands its horizons, enabling all kinds of new data types, analytics, and optimization techniques for the best performance and availability on the market.

About Dave Beulke

Dave Beulke is an internationally recognized consultant, author and teacher known for his strategic expertise in database performance, data warehouses, and Internet applications. He provides data management strategies, architectures, advanced designs, and systems consulting. Dave is currently a member of the IBM DB2 Gold Consultant program, an IBM Champion, coauthor of past IBM z/OS DB2 DBA certification and business intelligence certification exams, past president of IDUG, and former instructor for The Data Warehouse Institute (TDWI). He writes a weekly blog at *www.davebeulke. com*. Dave helps his clients improve their strategic direction, designs innovative solutions, dramatically improves performance, and reduces CPU demand, saving clients millions within their mainframe, UNIX®, and Microsoft® Windows® environments.

Cuneyt Goksu, VBT

The implementation of packages in DB2 V2.3 was a great milestone; it changed plan management from design and operational points. Online reorg and data sharing implementations provided superior availability to applications. The story of stored procedures from WLM managed to native SQL changed the whole picture of application design. Each and every day, customers are moving more business logic inside the DB2 engine.

DB2 for z/OS is the golden standard of RDBMSs. It's designed to execute mixed workloads, operate 24x7 with high performance, and provide great scalability design options. Over the years, its functions and features have been enhanced according to industry trends, needs, and hardware enhancements. z/OS and LUW versions are getting closer from a functional and design point of view. For each and every type of application or business segment that requires superior DBMS support, DB2 provides it at every level—from DB2 Express-C to DB2 for z/OS.

DB2 is still around because data is a business's most valuable asset, and DB2 is the best DBMS engine in the world for keeping data secure and serving it 24x7. It is still around because it is used not only for legacy OLTP and decision-support applications but also for GIS, business and predictive analysis, big data implementations, and more.

About Cuneyt Goksu

Cuneyt Goksu is Principal Information Management Consultant at VBT. He has worked with DB2 for more than 20 years. Since 2001, Cuneyt has worked as a DB2 SME and consultant focused on DB2 installation and migration, subsystem and application performance and tuning, security health checks, infrastructure design reviews, data and application modeling, data sharing implementations, modernization and database migrations, integration and federation projects, DB2 tool implementations, and DB2 training. A certified IBM solutions expert, Cuneyt holds many IBM Information Management Technical and Sales certifications. He has been an active member of the IDUG community since 2003 and is currently a member of IDUG BOD and leader of the Turkish DB2 User Group. Cuneyt is an IBM Information Champion, an IBM DB2 Gold Consultant, an Authorized DB2 Training Partner, and a member of IBM Academic Initiative Program. He holds an MBA and an MS in computer science.

Sheryl Larsen, Sheryl M. Larsen, Inc.

I graduated college in 1994, and at my first job DB2 V1 fell into my lap. SQL performance consulting has been a passion of mine ever since. I love showing off the advanced technology of the optimizer and SQL features that can handle the most complex of business questions. My clients are moving more and more data and applications to DB2, not less and less, due to the sophistication and synergy of DB2 with the hardware it runs on. Appliances are the future of DB2 in the Data Explosion world, with DB2 seamlessly integrating with Netezza today and with many more appliances to come.

About Sheryl Larsen

Sheryl M. Larsen is an internationally recognized researcher, consultant, and lecturer specializing in DB2. She owns Sheryl M. Larsen, Inc. (*www.smlsql.com*), a firm specializing in advanced DB2 consulting and education. Sheryl is known for her extensive expertise in SQL, and her firm performs detailed DB2 performance reviews for many clients worldwide. Sheryl has more than 25 years' experience in DB2, has published many articles, and is coauthor of *DB2 Answers!* (Osborne/McGraw-Hill, 1999). She is an IBM Champion, an IDUG Hall of Fame Speaker, and a longtime member of IBM's DB2 Gold Consultants Program.

Daniel Luksetich, Independent Consultant

I can remember transforming from my third day on the job in 1990 when I accidentally dropped a production database to a DBA and application architect responsible for the creation of a very large DB2 database that routinely processed over 100 million transactions a day in 2004. I'm still excited about designing production DB2 tables that can process between 13,000 and 20,000 inserts per second!

Having worked with other RDBMSs, I can testify with confidence that DB2 is by far the most secure, stable, and tunable database engine available. The flexibility of the database designs that are capable in DB2 lends itself to spectacular performance regardless of the database size, content, or workload!

About Daniel Luksetich

Daniel L. Luksetich is an independent consultant who has worked with DB2 since 1990 and has been involved in many large implementations of DB2 in the United States and Europe. Dan works every day on some of the largest and most complex DB2 implementations in the world. He is a certified DB2 DBA, system administrator, and application developer and has worked on the teams that have developed the DB2 for z/OS certification exams. He is the author of several DB2-related articles as well as coauthor of *DB2 9 for z/OS Database Administration: Certification Study Guide* (MC Press, 2007) and *DB2 10 for z/OS Database Administration: Certification Study Guide* (MC Press, 2012). Dan is a frequent speaker at IDUG conferences in the United States and Europe, as well as at the IBM IOD annual conference in Las Vegas. He also volunteers as a member of IDUG's Content Committee.

Cristian Molaro, Independent DB2 Consultant

Back when we migrated to DB2 Version 6, we DBAs suspected that users were quickly justifying a lot of small incidents by blaming the "new DB2 version." When we moved to DB2 7, we announced the availability of the new version two weeks after the actual migration. Nobody reported a DB2-related issue in between. After the public notification, things suddenly, and suspiciously, started to fail because of the "new DB2 version." This was one case where we had to deal more with human expectations than with DB2 itself.

A very mature, 30 years young, state-of-the-art database management system is what makes DB2 so great and is the reason it is still around today. I could not ask for more in terms of keeping, exploiting, and protecting my most critical assets: enterprise information. During its years, DB2 has followed and defined the industry trends that set the rules of today's business game. DB2 for z/OS provides the ideal foundation to help you design and implement systems that are both secure and open, and it is ideally suited to answer today's enterprise challenges.

About Cristian Molaro

Cristian Molaro is an independent DB2 specialist and an IBM Gold Consultant. He was recognized as an IBM Champion in 2009, 2010, 2011, and 2012. Cristian's main activity is linked to DB2 for z/OS administration and performance. He has presented papers at several international conferences and local user groups in Europe and North America and is coauthor of six IBM Redbooks related to DB2, including the recent *Optimizing DB2 Queries with IBM DB2 Analytics Accelerator for z/OS*. Cristian is part of the IDUG EMEA Conference Planning Committee, where he works as the Marketing Team Leader. He is also Chairman of the DB2 LUW User Group BeLux and was recognized by IBM as "Top" EMEA Consultant at IDUG's 2011 EMEA DB2 Tech Conference.

Zeljen Stanic, CA, Inc.

The milestone I remember the most is in DB2 V2.3 when packages were introduced. Working with the plans within CICS® was not an easy task. With the introduction of packages, the DBA's job became much more productive.

Enterprises are storing ever-increasing amounts of data that must be accessible around-the-clock. Downtime or delayed processing due to performance bottlenecks can cause more than a loss of productivity—it can mean losing customers. In today's business environment, organizations must ensure optimal performance for their databases and applications, and that's the reason why they have used DB2 as their preferred database for almost 30 years.

About Zeljen Stanic

Zeljen Stanic is a member of the DB management team at CA EMEA Technical Sales – Mainframe Center of Competence. He has been in IT more than 29 years, working in different positions including programmer, developer, and DBA for SQL/DS, DB2, and IMS. He has worked with SQL/DS since 1983 and with DB2 since 1989. Zeljen joined Platinum Technology in 1995 as a consultant for DB2 and DB2 tools. Following CA's acquisition of Platinum in 1999, he joined CA, where he supports DBM solutions and other mainframe solutions and works with DB2 customers in Austria, Croatia, the Czech Republic, Finland, Germany, Greece, Holland, Kuwait, Poland, Qatar, Russia, Saudi Arabia, Slovakia, Slovenia, Spain, and Turkey. Zeljen has spoken to numerous DB2 user groups and DB2 conferences and represents CA at EMEA IDUG CPC. He founded the SQLAdria Regional User Group in 1994.

Kurt Struyf, Suadasoft

One of the most memorable milestones of DB2 for z/OS is the introduction of data sharing in Version 4. It makes DB2 scalable beyond the reach of any other relational database. DB2 for z/OS will be around for a long time because it's extremely reliable, cutting edge, and dollar-for-dollar cheaper than its competitors.

About Kurt Struyf

Kurt Struyf is an independent DB2 consultant and IBM Champion. He has over 15 years of experience with DB2 for z/OS as (system) DBA. Besides his consultancy missions, Kurt teaches a wide range of DB2 classes all over the world and presents at several main conferences (IDUG, IOD, SQLAdria, to name a few). He is a member of the IDUG content committee. He works for Suadasoft in Luxembourg.

Julian Stuhler, Triton Consulting

Two key milestones stick in my mind. The first is the introduction of packages in V2.3—a fantastic enhancement that opened up many new possibilities for managing multiple versions of DB2 applications and provided the basis for my very first user group presentation. The second was when DB2 V5 first became available: I remember having a conversation with the great Roger Miller, who admitted that DB2 had finally become so complex and capable that he could no longer know and understand the internals for every part of it. If even he was struggling, I had no chance, and that meant I could relax and be content with focusing on a few specific areas.

There are many reasons why DB2 continues to be so successful 30 years after it was first introduced, but I think two are especially important. First, DB2 was the result of genuinely innovative research and a forward-thinking, robust design that provided an incredibly solid foundation for the future. Perhaps even more important, the product has proven time and time again that it can rapidly evolve to meet the changing needs of its users. There are countless examples of this, including the original transition from BI/decision-support workloads to OLTP (and now back again), addressing extreme scalability requirements with the introduction of data sharing in V4, becoming an "object relational" database in V6, and embracing XML in DB2 9. Every time there is a fundamental change in the requirements for an enterprise data store, DB2 has been there to provide a robust, well-engineered solution.

About Julian Stuhler

Julian Stuhler has been involved with DB2 for z/OS for more than 26 years and has worked with every release from V1R2 to DB2 10, first as a developer and later as a DBA, systems programmer, and consultant. He still has a pristine set of V1R3 manuals which he intends to re-read someday. Julian is an IBM Gold Consultant, an IBM Champion, and past president of the International DB2 Users Group (IDUG). Julian wanted to name his firstborn after the product, but fortunately his wife intervened.

Steve Thomas, BMC Software

The most important milestone for me in the development of DB2 has been the introduction of data sharing back in Version 4 toward the end of 1995. It took a few releases for this to become well established and used by more than the largest of customers, but in my mind it was the key feature that led us toward the high-availability and high-throughput system we all benefit from using today.

From my own perspective, the key factor in the success of DB2 is that DB2 is the database of choice on the platform of choice, zEnterprise®. No other combination can approach the performance, throughput, and availability that DB2 for z/OS provides—if you want proof, just look at what the world's leading companies overwhelmingly use for their strategic systems. When you add to this the availability of almost all the same features in the distributed platform version of DB2, the continual and sustained development of world-leading features such as XML, and the backing of IBM, then the selection of a database for any new enterprise business application should be a simple one.

About Steve Thomas

Steve Thomas is a Principal Consultant at BMC Software, based in the United Kingdom. He has worked with DB2 since Version 1.3 in 1989 and has been an IBM Champion for Information Management since 2009. A well-known speaker, Steve has presented on a wide range of topics at events across Europe. He has been a member of the IDUG EMEA Conference Planning Committee for the past seven years and also helps organize the U.K. local DB2 Regional User Group.

The Vision of DB2

IBM's DB2 leaders share their thoughts
about the strengths and future of DB2

Curt Cotner, IBM Fellow, Vice President and Chief Technology Officer for Database Servers

Technology, and the IT industry itself, has changed significantly over the past 30 years, and despite all those changes DB2 continues to be a critical element of the IT fabric in most large enterprises. People often ask what we did in DB2 to remain relevant over such a long period of time. In my mind, the single biggest thing we did was to establish a culture in our development team that ensures that our technical leaders are deeply engaged with the DB2 customer community. Unlike some of our competitors, the key designers of DB2 are all well known by our customers. They travel to meet you at conferences and come for on-site visits at your company's place of business. Many of you have worked with the DB2 designers one-on-one to work out solutions to the technology challenges you face, and often these end up as product enhancements in the next release of DB2. Many of our customers can personally identify multiple features in DB2 that they had a hand in designing. It is this tight interrelationship with our customers that allows DB2 to meet your data storage needs, and without your help in this area we would not have enjoyed this longevity.

I'd really like to take this opportunity to thank all of you for taking the time to work closely with us on these issues. It has been the single most important factor in making DB2 a successful and long-lived product.

About Curt Cotner

Curt Cotner is an IBM Fellow and a member of the IBM Academy of Technology. He is the Chief Technology Officer for the DB2 family and Informix® IDS database servers and has both management and technology oversight responsibility for all the client software offerings used with DB2 and IDS. This includes the client runtime APIs (JDBC, .NET, CLI, pureQuery, etc.) and the application development and administration tools offerings (IBM Data Studio). Prior to taking his current assignment, Curt was the chief architect for the DB2 for z/OS development team.

Jeff Josten, Distinguished Engineer, DB2 for z/OS Development

DB2 is still a vital product after 30 years mainly because of an extremely loyal and enthusiastic user community coupled with a highly skilled and experienced development team that listens and responds to customers. Another critical aspect to DB2's longevity that a lot of people probably don't appreciate is that the architectural foundations of the product are rock solid, and this allows us as the development team to easily (in most cases) extend DB2's capabilities to meet our customers' quickly evolving requirements. For this, we owe a big debt of gratitude to our product's creators, who had the foresight to understand that long-lasting software must be easily maintainable and extendable. DB2 continues to succeed because it has adapted over the years to rapidly changing technology and requirements, and it is very well positioned to continue in this mode for years to come.

About Jeff Josten

Jeff Josten is an IBM Distinguished Engineer and lead architect for DB2 for z/OS. He has worked in the DB2 Development organization at the IBM Silicon Valley Lab since 1985. Although he now covers all areas of DB2, his main areas of interest in the past have included data sharing, performance, availability, and recovery. Jeff owns several patents in the area of database technology and is a frequent speaker at DB2 user group meetings.

Ruiping Li, Senior Software Engineer in DB2 for z/OS Development

Clients around the world rely on DB2 for z/OS for its exceptional reliability, availability, serviceability, and security. It takes many talented and passionate professionals from all over the world to develop this product, and I am proud to have been a part of this team during the past decade. IBM continues to actively invest in DB2 with each release to improve performance, reduce cost, and introduce new capabilities, such as the new exciting product, IBM DB2 Analytics Accelerator. IBM DB2 Analytics Accelerator combines the strengths of both System z and Netezza systems, significantly reducing the CPU cost on System z, bringing lightning-fast performance to data-intensive and complex DB2 queries, and making DB2 the market leader for both OLTP and OLAP workloads. DB2 has been a successful product for 30 years, and I believe it will continue its success in the coming decades and continue to play an essential role in the changing the world of Information Management.

About Ruiping Li

Ruiping Li is a Senior Software Engineer in DB2 for z/OS Development at IBM's Silicon Valley Lab. She is currently a key designer for DB2 query acceleration support for the IBM DB2 Analytics Accelerator. Over the past decade, Ruiping has designed and implemented several key enhancements in DB2 for z/OS, such as optimistic locking support, timestamp with time zone support, pureXML index exploitation, index on expression, materialized query tables (MQTs), and multiple CCSID enhancements. Ruiping joined IBM in 2001 after graduating from Purdue University with a master's degree in computer science.

Dr. Pat Selinger, IBM Fellow and "The Mother of DB2"

More than three decades ago, as we built the research prototype that became the foundation for DB2, we were determined to prove that the relational databases were usable and could perform well. Wow! Did IBM ever prove that! DB2 has become a dynasty, with the world's leading performance, flexibility, and reliability. With its ability to enable ever richer types of data and support not only high-performance transactions but also deep analytics and data mining, DB2 provides the capabilities that are critical for Smarter Commerce®, Smarter Banking®, Smarter Manufacturing, Smarter Distribution, and the whole broad range of capabilities our customers need to build a Smarter Planet®.

About Pat Selinger

Dr. Pat Selinger is a world-renowned pioneer in relational database management and inventor of the technique of cost-based query optimization that has been adopted by nearly all relational database vendors and is now taught in virtually every university database course. She was a key member of the original System R team that created the first relational database research prototype. She established and led IBM's Database Technology Institute, considered one of the most successful examples of a fast technology pipeline from research to development, and personally has technical contributions in the areas of database optimization, data parallelism, distributed data, and unstructured data management. Dr. Selinger, now retired and consulting at IBM, was appointed an IBM Fellow (IBM's top technical honor) in 1994 and prior to her retirement held the position of IBM Vice President of Information Management Architecture and Technology. She is an ACM Fellow, a member of the National Academy of Engineering, and a Fellow of the American Academy of Arts and Sciences. Dr. Selinger has published more than 40 refereed papers, has received the ACM Systems Software Award for her work on System R, and has received the SIGMOD Innovation Award, the highest ACM award given in the area of data management. She is now a project consultant for IBM.

Kate Tennant, Senior Manager
of DB2 for z/OS Query Technology Development

I started with IBM in 1982. Since DB2 had not yet been announced, IBM was rather secretive about the project before I joined. All I knew was that I would be working on a pretty important software project for IBM. It sounded intriguing, and I thought it would be fun and exciting. Soon I learned that the project was DB2, and one year later it was announced to the world. I felt lucky and privileged to participate in the celebrations, since there were so many smart and talented people who had been working on the project for many years already. Now, 30 years later, DB2 is one of the most important and successful software products ever. Every day in the DB2 organization is still fun and exciting, and I still feel lucky and privileged to work with so many smart and talented people. I think it is safe to say that I won't last another 30 years in IBM, but I am sure that DB2 will still be here, managing the world's most important data and continuing to help make our world a "Smarter Planet."

About Kate Riley Tennant

Kate Riley Tennant is Senior Manager of DB2 for z/OS Query Technology Development. She leads a worldwide team of over 80 software engineers who are developing and servicing key components for DB2 for z/OS. Kate joined IBM in 1982 after graduating from California State Polytechnic University, Pomona, with a bachelor's degree in computer science and a minor in mathematics. She became a manager at IBM in 1987 and has managed many different teams at IBM's Silicon Valley Laboratory.

Revolution in IBM DB2 Performance: IBM DB2 Analytics Accelerator

by Namik Hrle, Ruiping Li, and Wolfgang Hengstler
IBM Boeblingen Development Laboratory and IBM Silicon Valley Lab

IBM DB2 Analytics Accelerator marks an inflection point in developing the DB2 technology. It brings lightning-fast performance to data-intensive and complex DB2 queries. This white paper covers the key DB2 Analytics Accelerator design and operational aspects that enable DB2 for IBM z/OS clients to benefit from faster performance, reduced CPU usage, and lower costs.

Abstract

DB2 Analytics Accelerator has been designed and developed as an internal DB2 component, so that in many aspects it is experienced as just another super-fast DB2 access path. The complex and data-intensive queries that characterize data warehouse, business intelligence, and analytics workloads can be now executed hundreds of times faster than before.

This paper answers several questions: What is business analytics, why is it important to your organization, and how does the IBM solution differ from others? Then, we address the unique DB2 Analytics Accelerator architecture that delivers a deep integration into DB2 and also takes advantage of the extremely fast, data-intensive query engine provided by IBM Netezza® technology. We also describe which query types qualify for the new "access path" and explain how to operate and monitor the accelerator.

Objectives

After defining business analytics and its importance to business needs, then addressing the key design and operational features, we will examine DB2 integration, when a query can be accelerated, and some performance monitoring features. Finally, we will discuss how DB2 Analytics Accelerator achieves high performance for the queries. Our goals are to

- Describe DB2 Analytics Accelerator architecture
- Learn how to use the accelerator, control acceleration, and maintain its content
- Learn how to interpret the new access path and monitor query acceleration

- Understand the query execution technology that powers the accelerator
- Learn which workloads and query types apply for the new access type

Introduction

Business analytics play a crucial role in today's workplace. The performance and cost of the DB2 Analytics Accelerator opens up unprecedented opportunities for enterprises to make use of the data on the IBM System z platform. Customers have seen dramatic improvement in the response times of the qualifying queries in some real, production-sized benchmarks. Running DB2 Analytics Accelerator on System z can result in some significant reductions in CPU usage. Of course, individual results will vary and depend on many other factors.

What Is Business Analytics? Timely, Accurate, and Secure Access to Business Information

Since the early days of data warehousing, the common statement from every vendor and pundit was that decision systems and transactional systems were vastly different and required separate platforms. Those days are over!

With the wealth of data available today, organizations are no longer willing to relegate information to the back office. Modern organizations are demanding access to customer purchase histories, customer behaviors, and trends of product sales at the time of contact—at the time of sale. This creates new challenges, because it is not enough for an enterprise to capture this data, but to process and transform these massive amounts of data into actionable knowledge. And this needs to be done quickly while the information is still relevant.

Data transformed into intelligence gives you more than a window into your current operations. It provides a likely view of the future—what is just around the corner and even further down the road. It helps leaders know with confidence all that has happened, is happening, and might happen to every aspect of the enterprise. Spotting the key patterns, extracting critical insights from data, and taking latency and cost out of making and implementing the right decision is what is defining industry leaders.

The world we live in today is increasingly instrumented, interconnected, and intelligent. We are experiencing a revolution, and information is at the heart of it. Businesses that are taking advantage of this new wealth of information are able to make more intelligent decisions and are rising to the top. They're managing large volumes of information in real time, incorporating analytics and predictive modeling, pervasively collecting and sharing information across the entire value chain, and speeding time to value by delivering trusted, accurate, and timely information to the right decision makers.

A company's survival can depend on the age of the data used to obtain an answer to critical business questions. With slow sales cycles, cutbacks, reluctant clients, and intense competition, business leaders are really feeling the heat to act and act fast, but a single bad decision today can be disastrous.

So what is the key to working smarter? It is having the right information and insight at the right time to drive smarter business outcomes. Working smarter means that your front-line business leaders receive timely information to uncover the new revenue opportunities and identify which product or service offerings are most likely to address the market requirement. It means business analysts can quickly access the right data points to evaluate key performance and revenue indicators in building successful corporate growth strategies. And, it means corporate risk and compliance units can recognize potential regulatory, reputational, and operational risks before they become realities.

The DB2 Analytics Accelerator gives your organization the speed to create the insights it needs to work smarter in this challenging environment. By putting the right answers in the hands of your decision makers immediately, DB2 Analytics Accelerator puts your business in the best position to quickly adapt and grow to answer the questions of tomorrow.

How Business Analytics Can Help Your Organization

Many organizations realize the benefit of improving business outcomes and improved decision making. The use of business intelligence and analytic applications is well understood to help make smarter decisions, achieve better results, and gain a deeper understanding of trends, opportunities, weaknesses, and threats. Organizations want to further analyze their data to gain additional insights into their business.

Today, however, the enterprise warehouse environment of an organization is facing many challenges. One such challenge is that the amount of data being stored in a typical warehouse environment is increasing. As the amount of data increases and sometimes the format of this data changes, the warehouse and end-user experience can be affected. It can become challenging for an organization to see the right information in an appropriate format and in the right timeframe for it to use in its analysis and decision-making process. Moving large amounts of data from disparate source systems to a warehouse can be a resource-intensive task. The increasing amount of data in some warehouses can also further affect any longer-running queries and reports that might exist in an organization. These slow-running queries, when executed with other mixed online transaction processing (OLTP) and online analytical processing (OLAP) workloads, can negatively affect the experience of existing users and cause further lack of acceptance for potential new users. Combine this with typical corporate priorities to become more productive, agile, and innovative, and it becomes more challenging to deliver on the promises of data warehousing and business analytics.

For many organizations, the concept that some of their longer-running DB2 for z/OS queries can be routed to an accelerator for processing is a plus. These queries may be in the form of batch SQL jobs or may be generated by means of corporate analytic and business intelligence (BI) tools—for example, ad hoc reporting from IBM Cognos® BI. The query accelerator available for DB2 for z/OS, which makes use of IBM Netezza technology, can make a big difference in the execution time of an analytic and warehouse type of workload. Combining the benefits of both DB2 for z/OS (for OLTP-type queries) and DB2 Analytics Accelerator (for longer-running analysis queries) ensures that resources are shared appropriately for all warehouse users.

The DB2 Analytics Accelerator would likely benefit an organization that fit one of the following profiles:

- Wants to undertake a new reporting initiative on IBM System z to gain more insights
- Wants to consolidate disparate data to its existing System z platform while benefiting from integrated operational BI
- Wants to modernize an existing data warehouse and BI workload on System z

These types of organizations, with the appropriate workload, would likely see their elapsed time for longer-running queries being significantly reduced. They would also likely see their CPU usage on the mainframe being reduced, allowing DB2 for z/OS to focus on efficiently running their OLTP queries. Other benefits for these organization profiles are discussed in the following sections.

New System z BI initiative to gain more insight

This profile describes a System z organization that has identified a new reporting or operational BI initiative to analyze data that is not being currently analyzed. The organization would like to gain insights into the data and its business, while benefiting from having accelerated performance for complex analytics and queries. In this situation, it makes sense to use the DB2 Analytics Accelerator component for DB2 for z/OS. BI and analytic applications such as Cognos BI only need to connect to DB2 for z/OS and can still benefit from query acceleration.

The benefits of using DB2 Analytics Accelerator for a new reporting or operational BI initiative on System z include:

- Improved data insights for the organization's business users and business processes
- Performance, availability, and scalability benefits by blending System z and the DB2 Analytics Accelerator
- Acceleration benefits that are transparent to DB2 applications
- Simplicity and time to value for new mixed BI workload initiatives (OLTP and OLAP and analytics)

Consolidating disparate data to System z

This profile describes an organization that has created its data warehouse on System z and also has a number of disparate data marts (or islands of data) scattered around the organization, where some of its workload queries are executed. Some of these silos of information may be custom-built applications, which typically require ongoing maintenance and modification. There may be only a select few in the organization who are able to maintain or use some of these silos, and reporting might require some manual data manipulation. The organization might have identified some potential benefits if some of the data flows and transformations to and from System z were eliminated, and if the organization wants a high performance integrated OLTP and BI analysis environment.

This type of organization could be facing any of the following challenges:

- There are multiple versions of the "truth." This could include different applications providing different answers for the same information request, or different areas of the organization that own their own reporting data marts and apply their own interpretation of business rules.
- Corporate reporting and business analysis requires the use of multiple applications.
- Administration and management of multiple platforms and complex data integration processes are required.
- The value of consolidating data into a single easily managed platform (integrated OLTP and analysis/OLAP) has been identified, but some concerns may exist as to how analytic and traditional business intelligence workloads may perform on the mainframe.
- Deploying new data marts within the organization takes too long. Business benefit and value to the organization is not achieved in a timely manner.

The benefits of consolidating data on System z and including query acceleration with DB2 Analytics Accelerator are the same performance benefits mentioned in the previous organization profile. In addition, this type of organization might realize benefits including:

- Consolidated islands of data to a single secure data environment, providing "one version of the truth"
- An integrated OLTP and BI environment, enabling application queries that are required to use more real-time data
- Fewer servers to administer and less-competitive platforms
- The possible elimination of some network components, meaning fewer points of failure
- The enablement of data analytics consolidation through DB2 Analytics Accelerator
- The benefits of System z performance, scalability, and reliability combined with the accelerated performance of DB2 Analytics Accelerator
- The use of DB2 Analytics Accelerator to improve analysis workload performance, rather than requiring additional System z Integrated Information Processors to support the consolidated data warehouse environment

Modernizing an existing traditional BI workload

This profile describes an organization that has already created their data warehouse on System z. The warehouse contains historical data and coexists with many of the organization's operational applications. The organization wishes to improve the performance of its existing BI and analytic workload.

Organizational challenges may include:

- Difficulty in extending the use of operational data for business analysis, embedding operational analytics in other applications, or daily business intelligence reporting.
- Long-running DB2 for z/OS queries. These queries may be executed from a BI environment and provide important business information. Currently, the queries can be scheduled in batch processes overnight so that they don't affect corporate users during the day. However, the overnight schedules could mean that information is not available in a timely manner—or that the full potential of having this information for other business processes is not realized.
- Forgotten queries, which due to performance issues are no longer executed. Some of these queries may have already been through exhaustive tuning efforts without success. If they were able to run successfully in a timely manner, the results could provide important decision-making information.
- Performance challenges with complex and ad hoc queries. Users, when building ad hoc queries through BI tools, may not realize the impact of their ad hoc querying.

The benefits of query acceleration using DB2 Analytics Accelerator for this organization include:

- Significantly improved query performance and execution time for individual queries or overall workloads, freeing up millions of instructions per second (MIPS) and storage space, therefore reducing processing cost
- The ability to execute queries that were either forgotten or blocked previously by the administrator due to performance issues
- Increased organizational agility by being able to more rapidly respond with immediate, accurate information and deliver new insights to business users
- Consolidated reporting on System z, where the majority of the data being analyzed lives, while retaining System z security and reliability

Impact on total cost of ownership (TCO)

In our scenario, query and reporting constitutes the DB2 dominant workload. In general, the DB2 Analytics Accelerator potential to effectively improve response times and possibly reduce costs by a CPU reduction is related to the costing model in effect in your organization. Most customers use monthly license charge (MLC) software based on a four-hour rolling peak average across a month. You must have a clear understanding of the way CPU is used and how CPU use for dynamic queries is reflected in your TCO.

Key Design and Operational Features

Figure 1.1 describes an IBM DB2 system, including applications, tools, and DB2 itself. Inside DB2 we have some familiar components, such as the Data Manager, Buffer Manager, Log Manager, Internal Release Lock Manager (IRLM), Relational Data System

(RDS), and more. Applications interact with DB2 through the application interfaces using SQL. Database administrators interact with DB2 through the operation interfaces, such as commands and utilities or performance monitoring and tuning tools.

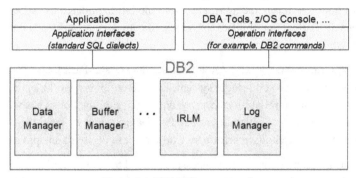

Figure 1.1: IBM DB2 components

Figure 1.2 illustrates that IBM now has a new "virtual" DB2 component, called IBM DB2 Analytics Accelerator. DB2 Analytics Accelerator has hardware and software components, based on IBM Netezza technology, used to accelerate complex queries that typically are seen in analytics applications.

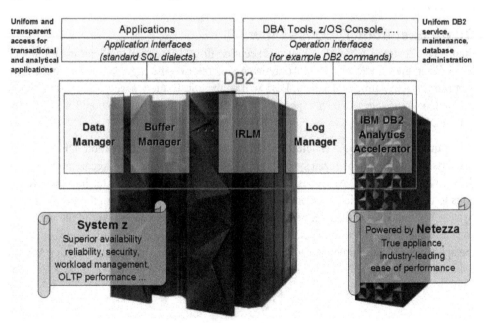

Figure 1.2: IBM DB2 becomes a Hybrid Database Management System

The IBM PureData™ System for Analytics appliance, connected to DB2, is enhanced to act as a DB2 accelerator. And DB2 has been enhanced with query acceleration to execute queries in DB2 Analytics Accelerator. DB2 Analytics Accelerator provides lightning-fast query performance transparently to the DB2 applications—at an affordable price. It opens up endless possibilities for new applications and workloads on data stored in DB2 for z/OS in enterprises.

Deep integration between DB2 Analytics Accelerator and DB2 for z/OS combines the best of both worlds into one single system. DB2 for z/OS is a world leader in OLTP, with superior availability, reliability, security, and serviceability. It also has world-class workload management capabilities. The PureData System for Analytics appliance provides superb data warehouse performance and the ease of use of an appliance.

Using it as an accelerator, it's not necessary to tend to administrative processes as with a standalone unit. You deal with data integrity and security on z/OS. DB2 Analytics Accelerator simply retains a copy of the data you want to accelerate the queries on and executes the queries for DB2.

DB2 Analytics Accelerator is administrated using a set of DB2 stored procedures. Query acceleration is viewed as a new query access path for DB2 which can be seen in the EXPLAIN output.

Query Execution Process Flow

Figure 1.3 illustrates a high-level query execution flow. There is an application on the left, DB2 in the middle, and DB2 Analytics Accelerator on the right. When the application submits a dynamic SQL query, DB2 will analyze it. If query acceleration is not enabled, or if the query does not qualify for acceleration, it will be executed locally within DB2.

If query acceleration is enabled and the query qualifies for acceleration, DB2 converts the query into Netezza syntax and routes it to DB2 Analytics Accelerator through an internal DB2 Analytics Accelerator to IBM DRDA® requestor interface. It talks to the DB2 Analytics Accelerator DRDA server on the SMP host in the PureData System for Analytics appliance, which completes the query execution within the appliance box and sends the result back to DB2 through DRDA. And the result is sent out to the application. The figure also shows the heartbeat messages from DB2 Analytics Accelerator to DB2, with DB2 Analytics Accelerator availability and performance indicators.

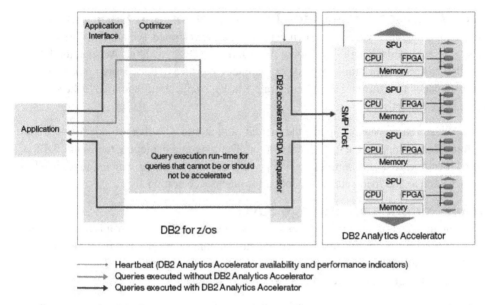

-------→ Heartbeat (DB2 Analytics Accelerator availability and performance indicators)
———→ Queries executed without DB2 Analytics Accelerator
━━━→ Queries executed with DB2 Analytics Accelerator

Figure 1.3: Query execution process flow

DB2 Analytics Accelerator Content Maintenance

Query acceleration by DB2 Analytics Accelerator is a new access path for DB2, just like an index access path. To enable this access path, you need to set up and enable query acceleration. One of the key steps is to have a copy of the table data in DB2 Analytics Accelerator so the queries can execute against them.

You define tables to be accelerated and then load the data from DB2 into DB2 Analytics Accelerator. You can refresh the data content periodically. The accelerator uses the DB2 UNLOAD utility to unload data, in parallel, to UNIX System Services (USS) pipes. DB2 Analytics Accelerator will read the data and convert it into a LOAD to the PureData System for Analytics appliance.

Partitions belonging to the same table can be loaded in parallel, with a user-controlled degree of parallelism to balance CPU and load throughput. Refresh or updates are done on a "per table," "per partition," or incremental basis.

Incremental update is a capability that enables tables on the DB2 Analytics Accelerator to be continually updated throughout the day. This technology reads the log of the database residing on DB2 for z/OS and applies those updates to the DB2 Analytics Accelerator. With this feature enabled, queries routed to the DB2 Analytics Accelerator will operate against a near real-time version of the data. It enables clients to dramatically lower the latency of data, letting decisions be made based on the most up-to-date information available. Customers use this feature when the workload being accelerated requires high currency of data for applications such as operational analytics. Incremental update is part of the accelerator's integrated appliance form factor.

DB2 Analytics Accelerator Table Definition and Deployment

Before loading data, you need to define tables to be accelerated. All administrative tasks are achieved through DB2 stored procedures for DB2 Analytics Accelerator. DB2 Analytics Accelerator Studio provides a graphical interface to these stored procedures and convenience in performing the administrative tasks. Applications can invoke the stored procedures directly.

The stored procedures update the pseudo catalog tables, which provide the necessary information to support the query acceleration. Defining and deploying tables into DB2 Analytics Accelerator is simple. You simply identify the tables for which queries need to be accelerated and load data and enable it for query acceleration.

High-Performance Storage Saver

Most analytical systems are based on data in which over 95 percent of it is historical and, therefore, static. A retailer, for instance, might maintain seven years of past sales histories that contain every transaction for every product sold to each customer. Because this data is historical, it generally is not subject to revision or updates.

High-performance storage savers reduce the cost of storing, managing, and processing this type of data. Organizations can select those tables or table partitions and not require them to consume space within the System z storage environment. All of the data is still maintained in the DB2 directory, and all the queries that target that data are now only directed to the accelerator. Not only does this dramatically reduces storage costs on System z, but it also enables organization to substantially increase the amount of history maintained for each subject area.

Connectivity Options

Depending on your situation, you can connect multiple DB2 systems to a single DB2 Analytics Accelerator to share the capacity. Or, a single DB2 system can connect to multiple DB2 Analytics Accelerators to achieve load sharing and redundancy for high reliability. You can also connect multiple DB2 systems to multiple DB2 Analytics Accelerators and "mix and match" them.

There is great flexibility for DB2 systems.

Disaster Recovery Considerations

Disaster recovery can be extended to DB2 Analytics Accelerator connected to DB2. This is a configuration with two data-sharing group members, each attached with a DB2 Analytics Accelerator. The diagram in Figure 1.4 shows how applications 1, 2, and 3 are connected to member 1 and are using DB2 Analytics Accelerator 1. Applications 4 and 5 are on the other member.

In case the member 1 system is down, applications 1, 2, and 3 can reconnect to member 2. By redeploying (loading and enabling) tables for applications 1, 2, and 3 on

DB2 Analytics Accelerator 2, you can use DB2 Analytics Accelerator 2 as the accelerator for them. Tables can be loaded into multiple DB2 Analytics Accelerators. And the system can be up and running with all the applications. To shorten disaster recovery time, tables can be loaded redundantly into multiple DB2 Analytics Accelerators. Then, only enabling is needed for the switch.

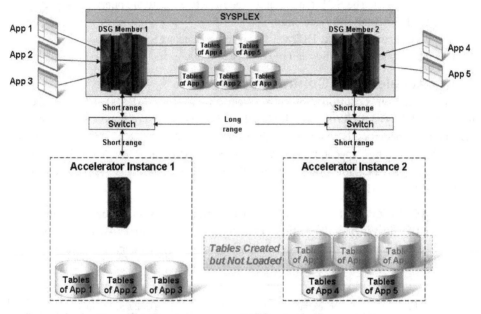

Figure 1.4: Disaster recovery – Table loaded in one accelerator

DB2 integration

Deep integration of DB2 Analytics Accelerator with DB2 has affected many DB2 components. This list identifies some of the more visible areas related to DB2 Analytics Accelerator:

- Optimizer and routing criteria
- Distributed data facility/Distributed Relational Database Architecture (DDF/DRDA)
- System parameters
- Special register
- Explain
- Dynamic statement cache
- Instrumentation
- DB2 commands
- DB2 Analytics Accelerator administrative stored procedures

Query Acceleration Criteria

There are three parts in the query acceleration criteria:

1. **Environment/setup:** The DB2 system, DRDA protocol, and query package.
2. **The query itself:** INSERT from a SELECT statement or a dynamic read-only SELECT statement; references only tables that are deployed in the same accelerator. The SQL functionality required to execute the query is supported by the DB2 Analytics Accelerator.
3. **Acceleration check:** DB2 verifies whether acceleration will speed up the query based on the heuristics and the estimated query cost.

Query Acceleration Control Knobs

Query acceleration is controlled by both system parameters (ZPARMs) and a new special register, CURRENT QUERY ACCELERATION. Following is a list of three ZPARM parameters and the special register setting for the query acceleration. The ZPARMs apply at the system level. The new special register can be used to control an individual SQL statement. It inherits the default value from the QUERY_ACCELERATION ZPARM and can override the ZPARM setting.

- **ACCEL ZPARM**—Specifies whether accelerator servers can be used with the DB2 subsystem and how they are to be enabled and started. An accelerator server cannot be started unless it is enabled. To enable query acceleration, ACCEL should be set as AUTO or COMMAND.

Value	Description
NO	The accelerator servers cannot be used with the DB2 subsystem.
AUTO	The accelerator servers are automatically enabled and started when the DB2 subsystem is enabled.
COMMAND	The accelerator servers are automatically enabled when the DB2 subsystem is started. The accelerator servers can be started with the DB2 START ACCEL command.

- **ACCEL_LEVEL ZPARM**—Specifies which version of the accelerator DB2 is to use (required only for DB2 Version 9.1). To enable query acceleration, ACCEL_ LEVEL should be set to V2.

Value	Description
V1	The accelerator servers are to use IBM Smart Analytics Optimizer Version 1. V1 is the default.
V2	The accelerator servers are to use DB2 Analytics Accelerator.

- **QUERY_ACCELERATION ZPARM**—Determines the default value that is to be used for the CURRENT QUERY ACCELERATION special register.

Value	Description
NONE	No query is accelerated. NONE is the default.
ENABLE	The queries are accelerated only if DB2 determines that it is advantageous to do so. If there is an accelerator failure while a query is running, or the accelerator returns an error, DB2 returns a negative SQLCODE to the application.
ENABLE_WITH_FAILBACK	The queries are accelerated only if DB2 determines that it is advantageous to do so. If the accelerator returns an error during the PREPARE of first OPEN for the query, DB2 executes the query without the accelerator. If the accelerator returns an error during a FETCH or a subsequent OPEN, DB2 returns the error to the user, and does not execute the query.
ELIGIBLE	The queries are accelerated if they are eligible for acceleration. DB2 does not use cost information to determine whether to accelerate the queries. Queries that are not eligible for acceleration are executed by DB2. If there is an accelerator failure while a query is running, or the accelerator returns an error, DB2 returns a negative SQLCODE to the application.
ALL	The queries are accelerated if they are eligible for acceleration. DB2 does not use cost information to determine whether to accelerate the queries. Queries that are not eligible for acceleration are not executed by DB2, and an SQL error is returned. If there is an accelerator failure while a query is running, or the accelerator returns an error, DB2 returns a negative SQLCODE to the application.

- **CURRENT QUERY ACCELERATION special register**—The special register is used to override the QUERY_ACCELERATION ZPARM. It determines whether SQL queries are considered for query acceleration and indicates what DB2 does if the accelerator server fails. There are five possible values: NONE, ENABLE, ENABLE_WITH_FAILBACK, ELIGIBLE, and ALL (as described earlier). To enable query acceleration, CURRENT QUERY ACCELERATION should be set to a value other than NONE.

EXPLAIN Function

The DB2 EXPLAIN function is enhanced to provide basic information about accelerator usage. It tells whether a query qualifies for acceleration and, if not, why it is not qualified. The access path details associated with the query execution by the accelerator are provided independently of DB2 EXPLAIN by the IBM DB2 Analytics Accelerator Studio.

When a query is accelerated, for each query, regardless the number of query blocks that the query contains, the whole query has one row in both PLAN_TABLE and DSN_QUERYINFO_TABLE. PLAN_TABLE column ACCESSTYPE is 'A'. DSN_QUERYINFO_TABLE column QI_DATA contains the converted accelerator query text. If the query is not accelerated, REASON_CODE and QI_DATA columns provide details about why the query is not accelerated.

Note that the EXPLAIN tables can be populated with the above-described information even if no accelerator is connected to DB2. Specifying EXPLAINONLY on the START ACCEL command does not establish any communications with an actual accelerator, but it enables DB2 to consider the accelerator's presence in the access path selection process. This is the virtual accelerator feature. It is useful when the resource limit facility (RLF) limits the execution of some long-running queries and you want to find out whether these long-running queries qualify for acceleration.

Table 1.1 lists the columns in DSN_QUERYINFO_TABLE. The columns shown in italics contain information more specific to DB2 Analytics Accelerator enhancements.

Column name	Column contents
QUERYNO	A number that identifies the statement that is being explained.
QBLOCKNO	A number that identifies each query block within a query.
QINAME1	*If REASON_CODE = 0, the name of the accelerator.*
QINAME2	*If REASON_CODE = 0, the location of the accelerator.*
APPLNAME	The name of the application plan for the row. Applies only to embedded EXPLAIN statements that are executed from a plan or to statements that are explained when binding a plan. A blank indicates that the column is not applicable.
PROGNAME	The name of the program or package containing the statement being explained. Applies only to embedded EXPLAIN statements and to statements explained as the result of binding a plan or package. A blank indicates that the column is not applicable.
VERSION	The version identifier for the package. Applies only to an embedded EXPLAIN statement executed from a package or to a statement that is explained when binding a package. A blank indicates that the column is not applicable.
COLLID	The collection ID for the package. Applies only to an embedded EXPLAIN statement that is executed from a package or to a statement that is explained when binding a package. A blank indicates that the column is not applicable.
GROUP_MEMBER	The member name of the DB2 that executed EXPLAIN. The column is blank for non-data sharing.
SECTNOI	The section number of the statement.
SEQNO	The sequence number in the table.
EXPLAIN_TIME	The time at which the statement is processed. This time is the same as the BIND_TIME column in PLAN_TABLE.
TYPE	*The type of the output for this row. "A" means that this row is for a query that DB2 attempts to run on an accelerator server. The value in column REASON_CODE indicates the outcome.*
REASON_CODE	*If 0, the query qualifies for acceleration. Otherwise, the query cannot be accelerated. More details in Table 1.2.*
QI_DATA	*If REASON_CODE = 0, the text of the converted SQL statement (sent to DB2 Analytics Accelerator). Otherwise, the description of the reason for not qualifying for acceleration.*
SERVICE_INFO	IBM internal use only.
QB_INFO_ROWID	IBM internal use only.

Table 1.1: DSN_QUERYINFO_TABLE columns

Table 1.2 lists the REASON_CODE values that tell why a query is not qualified for acceleration.

Value	Description
0	Query qualifies for acceleration.
1	No active accelerator was found when EXPLAIN was executed.
2	The special register CURRENT QUERY ACCELERATION is set to NONE.
3	The query is a DB2 short-running query, or rerouting to the accelerator is not considered advantageous.
4	The query is not read-only.
5	The query is running under the private protocol.
6	The cursor is defined as a scrollable or rowset cursor.
7	The query refers to multiple encoding schemes.
8	The query FROM clause specifies a data-change-table-reference.
9	The query contains a correlated table expression.
10	The query contains a recursive common table expression reference.
11	The query contains an unsupported expression. QI_DATA contains the expression text.
12	The query references table *table-name* that is either not defined in the accelerator, or, if the table is defined, is not enabled for query re-routing.
13	The accelerator *accelerator-name* containing the tables of the query is not started.
14	The column *column-name* referenced in the query is altered in DB2 after the data is loaded in the accelerator.
15	The query references a DB2 10 new SQL feature.
16	The query is not from a package.
900–999	IBM internal use.

Table 1.2: REASON_CODE values indicating why a query is not qualified for acceleration

System-Scope Instrumentation

Instrumentation has been enhanced to include accelerator-related information. Figure 1.5 shows a sample of the STATISTICS REPORT from IBM OMEGAMON®.

```
1   LOCATION: PMOV91A              OMEGAMON XE FOR DB2 PERFORMANCE EXPERT (V5R1)              PAGE: 1-23
       GROUP: N/P                         STATISTICS REPORT - LONG              REQUESTED FROM: NOT SPECIFIED
      MEMBER: N/P                                                                          TO: NOT SPECIFIED
   SUBSYSTEM: V91A                                                              INTERVAL FROM: 09/06/11 21:49:41.35
 DB2 VERSION: V9                                        SCOPE: MEMBER                       TO: 09/06/11 23:41:50.70


 ---- HIGHLIGHTS ----------------------------------------------------------------------------------------------
 INTERVAL START  : 09/06/11 21:49:41.35    SAMPLING START: 09/06/11 21:49:41.35   TOTAL THREADS        :    76.00
 INTERVAL END    : 09/06/11 23:41:50.70    SAMPLING END  : 09/06/11 23:41:50.70   TOTAL COMMITS        :   109.00
 INTERVAL ELAPSED:    1:50:52.248034       OUTAGE ELAPSED:       1:17.097273      DATA SHARING MEMBER:      N/A


 ZGRYPHON          ACCELERATOR      QUANTITY     ZGRYPHON          CONTINUED           QUANTITY
 ---------------------------------- --------     ------------------------------- --------------------

 CONNECTS                              2.00      AVG QRY QUEUE LEN (3 HRS)             0.00
 REQUESTS                              9.00      AVG QRY QUEUE LEN (24 HRS)            0.00
 REQUESTS TIMED OUT                    0.00      HWM QRY QUEUE LENGTH                  0.00
 REQUESTS FAILED                       0.00      DATA SKEW                            0.00
 BYTES SENT                         4630.00      AVG QUEUE WAIT ELAPSED TIME     0.000000
 BYTES RECEIVED                   224887.00      MAX QUEUE WAIT ELAPSED TIME     0.000000
 MESSAGES SENT                        27.00
 MESSAGES RECEIVED                    27.00      PROCESSING CAPACITY                  0.00
 BLOCKS SENT                           0.00      PROCESSORS                           1.62
 BLOCKS RECEIVED                       5.00
 ROWS SENT                             0.00      QUERY REQUESTS SUCCESSFUL            1.00
 ROWS RECEIVED                         0.00      QUERY REQUESTS FAILED                1.00
                                                 QUERY REQUESTS INVALID               0.00
 SVCS TCP/IP ELAPSED TIME         7.036035
 ACCELERATOR CPU TIME             0.000000       SHR MEM WORKER NODES    (MB)         0.00
 ACCELERATOR ELAPSED TIME         0.000001         AVG IN USE            (MB)         0.00
 ACCELERATOR WAIT TIME            0.000000         MAX IN USE            (MB)         0.00

 CUR ACTIVE REQUESTS                   0.00      DISK STORAGE AVAILABLE  (MB)     98842.63
 MAX ACTIVE REQUESTS                   0.00        IN USE                (MB)         0.81
                                                   IN USE FOR DB         (MB)         0.81
                                                 DATA SLICES                          3.25

                                                 MEM COORD AVG IN USE    (MB)         0.00
                                                 MEM WORKER AVG IN USE   (MB)         0.00
```

Figure 1.5: IBM OMEGAMON statistics reports

Thread-Scope Instrumentation

Figure 1.6 shows the accounting report for user ADMF001 plan db2jcc_a and the accelerator XGRYPHON activity.

```
LOCATION: PMOV91A                OMEGAMON XE FOR DB2 PERFORMANCE EXPERT (V5R1)              PAGE: 1-7
   GROUP: N/P                            ACCOUNTING REPORT - LONG              REQUESTED FROM: NOT SPECIFIED
  MEMBER: N/P                                                                             TO: NOT SPECIFIED
SUBSYSTEM: V91A                           ORDER: PRIMAUTH-PLANNAME             INTERVAL FROM: 09/06/11 21:52:08.31
DB2 VERSION: V9                           SCOPE: MEMBER                                    TO: 09/06/11 23:43:26.65

PRIMAUTH: ADMF001  PLANNAME: db2jcc_a

---- DISTRIBUTED ACTIVITY ----------------------------------------------------------------------------------------
SERVER                : XGRYPHON          CONVERSATIONS INITIATED:    1.00    #COMMIT(1)SENT:        0    MESSAGES SENT        :      14.33
PRODUCT ID            : AQT               #CONVERSATIONS QUEUED  :       0    #ROLLB(1)SENT:        0    MESSAGES RECEIVED:          14.33
METHOD                : DRDA PROTOCOL     CONVERSATION TERMINATED:     N/A    SQL SENT     :     6.33    BYTES SENT           :    2403.33
REQUESTER ELAP.TIME:      2.402285        #RLUP THREADS          :     N/A    ROWS RECEIVED:     0.00    BYTES RECEIVED   : 138728.33
SERVER ELAPSED TIME:          N/A                                                                       BLOCKS RECEIVED  :        3.33
SERVER CPU TIME    :          N/A
DBAT WAITING TIME  :          N/A
#DDF ACCESSES      :            3

#COMMIT(2) SENT    :            0         #BACKOUT(2) SENT   :         0    #BKOUT(2) R.R:        0    #LASTAGN.SENT        :         0
                                          SUCCESSFULLY ALLOC.CONV:   N/A    TRANSACT.SENT:     1.00    STMT BOUND AT SER:         N/A
                                          MAX OPEN CONVERSATIONS :   N/A    MSG.IN BUFFER:     0.00    #FORGET RECEIVED :           0
                                          #CONT->LIM.BL.FTCH SWCH:   N/A    #PREPARE SENT:        0
                                          #COMMIT(2) RESP.RECV.  :     0

ACCELERATOR   IDENTIFIER                 ACCELERATOR           TOTAL VALUE    TOTAL TIME      AVERAGE VALUE   AVERAGE TIME
-----------   ----------                 -----------           -----------    ----------      -------------   ------------
PRODUCT       AQT02010                   OCCURRENCES                     3                              1.00
SERVER        XGRYPHON                   CONNECTS                        3                              1.00
                                         REQUESTS                       16                              5.33
                                         TIMED OUT                       0                              0.00
                                         FAILED                          0                              0.00
                                         SENT
                                         BYTES                        7210                           2403.33
                                         MESSAGES                       43                             14.33
                                         BLOCKS                          0                              0.00
                                         ROWS                            0                              0.00
                                         RECEIVED
                                         BYTES                      416185                         138728.33
                                         MESSAGES                       43                             14.33
                                         BLOCKS                         10                              3.33
                                         ROWS                            0                              0.00

                                         ELAPSED TIME
                                         SVCS TCP/IP               7.206857                              2.402286
                                         ACCUM ACCEL               0.000061                              0.000020
                                         CPU TIME
                                         SVCS TCP/IP               0.015023                              0.005008
                                         ACCUM ACCEL               0.000000                              0.000000
                                         WAIT TIME
                                         ACCUM ACCEL               0.000000                              0.000000
```

Figure 1.6: IBM OMEGAMON accounting report

DB2 Analytics Accelerator Administrative Stored Procedures

Table 1.3 lists the DB2 Analytics Accelerator administrative stored procedures. Most of these stored procedures can be invoked from applications to automate some tasks, such as refresh DB2 Analytics Accelerator data after ETL load.

Stored procedure	Description
ACCEL_ADD_ACCELERATOR	Pair an accelerator to a DB2 subsystem
ACCEL_TEST_CONNECTION	Check the connectivity from DB2 procedures to the accelerator
ACCEL_REMOVE_ACCELERATOR	Remove an accelerator from a DB2 subsystem and clean up resources on the accelerator
ACCEL_UPDATE_CREDENTIALS	Renew the credentials (authentication token) in the accelerator
ACCEL_ADD_TABLES	Add a set of tables to the accelerator
ACCEL_ALTER_TABLES	Alter table definitions for a set of tables on the accelerator (only distribution and organizing keys)
ACCEL_REMOVE_TABLES	Remove a set of tables from the accelerator
ACCEL_GET_TABLES_INFO	List a set of tables on the accelerator together with detail information
ACCEL_LOAD_TABLES	Load data from DB2 into a set of tables on the accelerator
ACCEL_SET_TABLES_ACCELERATION	Enable or disable a set of tables for query offloading

continued

Stored procedure	Description
ACCEL_CONTROL_ACCELERATOR	Control the accelerator tracing, collecting trace, and detail of the accelerator (software level, etc.)
ACCEL_UPDATE_SOFTWARE	Update software on the accelerator (transfer versioned software packages or apply an already transferred package; new: also list software both on the z/OS and the accelerator side)
ACCEL_GET_QUERY_DETAILS	Retrieve statement text and the query plan for a running or completed query that is routed to the DB2 accelerator
ACCEL_GET_QUERY_EXPLAIN	Generate and retrieve the DB2 accelerator explain output for a query
ACCEL_GET_QUERIES	Retrieve active and/or history query information from the accelerator
ACCEL_SET_TABLES_REPLICATION	Enable or disable incremental updates for one or more tables on an accelerator
ACCEL_GET_TABLES_DETAILS	Collect information about a set of tables with regard to data changes (consistency) or move operations with the High Performance Storage Saver
ACCEL_ARCHIVE_TABLES	Move table partitions from DB2 for z/OS to a storage saver on an accelerator

Table 1.3: IBM DB2 Analytics Accelerator administrative stored procedures

DISPLAY ACCELerator Command

Figure 1.7 provides an example of the –DISPLAY ACCELERATOR command. The command shows a group scope status.

```
-DIS ACC(*) SCOPE(GROUP)
DSNX830I ) DSNX8CMD DISPLAY ACCELERATOR FOLLOWS -
ACCELERATOR                       MEMB   STATUS  REQUESTS ACTV QUED MAXQ
--------------------------------  ----  -------- -------- ---- ---- ----
BLINK1                            DB1A  STARTED    32769    2    5   23
BLINK1                            DB1B  STARTED    23456    1    0    2
BLINK1                            DB1C  STARTED      734    0    0    4
BLINK1                            DB1D  STARTED     9210    0    0    1
BLINK2                            DB1A  STOPPED    37235    1    7   17
BLINK2                            DB1B  STOPPED       47    0    0    0
BLINK2                            DB1C  STARTED        2    0    0    0
BLINK2                            DB1D  STOPPED        0    0    0    0
BLINK3                            DB1A  STARTED     3256    5   23   41
BLINK3                            DB1B  STOPPED       92    0    0    2
BLINK3                            DB1C  STARTED       87    0    0    7
BLINK3                            DB1D  STOPPED       21    0   11   11
DISPLAY ACCELERATOR REPORT COMPLETE
DSN9022I ) DSNX8CMD '-DISPLAY ACCEL' NORMAL COMPLETION
```

Figure 1.7: DISPLAY ACCELerator command

Figure 1.8 shows an example of the display of the active accelerator BLINK1 for DB1D.

```
-DIS ACC(BLINK1) LIST(ACTIVE) SCOPE(LOCAL) MEMBER(DB1D)

DSNX810I ) DSNX8CMD DISPLAY ACCEL FOLLOWS -
DSNX830I ) DSNX8CDA
ACCELERATOR                       MEMB  STATUS  REQUESTS ACTV QUED MAXQ
--------------------------------- ----  -------- -------- ---- ---- ----
BLINK1                            DB1D  STARTED     9210    7    5    9

LOCATION=ACCELERATOR1 HEALTHY

DETAIL STATISTICS
LEVEL = AQT02010
STATUS = ONLINE
FAILED QUERY REQUESTS = 3
AVERAGE QUEUE WAIT = 99
MAXIMUM QUEUE WAIT = 400
TOTAL NUMBER OF PROCESSORS = 4
AVERAGE CPU UTILIZATION ON COORDINATOR NODES = 45.00%
AVERAGE CPU UTILIZATION ON WORKER NODES = 40.00%
NUMBER OF ACTIVE WORKER NODES = 2
TOTAL DISK STORAGE AVAILABLE = 93000 MB
TOTAL DISK STORAGE IN USE = 56100 MB
DISK STORAGE IN USE FOR DATABASE = 36100 MB
DISPLAY ACCEL REPORT COMPLETE
DSN9022I ) DSNX8CMD '-DISPLAY ACCEL' NORMAL COMPLETION
```

Figure 1.8: Active accelerator display for BLINK1 for DB1D

Performance Considerations

Query acceleration:

- Consider tradeoffs when determining which workload or queries to offload. Speed-up factor and CPU savings will need to be weighed against query volume for maximum throughput.
- Keep DB2 table and index statistics up-to-date so that DB2 can make optimal DB2 Analytics Accelerator offloading decisions.
- Watch for queries that return large result sets, and push down data aggregation into the accelerator as applicable.

Loading data to PureData System for Analytics:

- Tune the AQT_MAX_UNLOAD_IN_PARALLEL Workload Manager (WLM) environment variable for the DB2 Analytics Accelerator load stored procedure, and weigh the available system CPU resources and number of optimal concurrent active threads (recommended maximum of 10 threads) on PureData System for Analytics for optimal load performance.
- Specify appropriate distribution and organizing keys for tables before loading the tables into PureData System for Analytics from the DB2 Analytics Accelerator client.

Powered by Netezza

DB2 Analytics Accelerator uses IBM Netezza technology as the accelerator. The PureData System for Analytics has a revolutionary design based on principles that have allowed it to provide an excellent price-to-performance ratio.

Figure 1.9 shows the four key components that make up the PureData System for Analytics:

- Symmetric multiprocessing (SMP) hosts
- Snippet blades (called S-Blades)
- Disk enclosures
- Network fabric (not shown in the illustration)

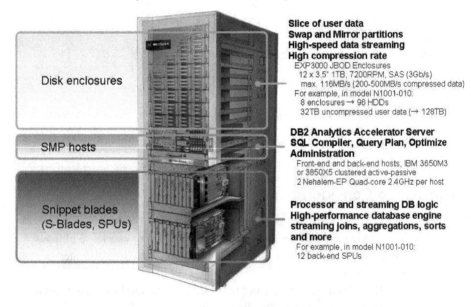

Figure 1.9: Accelerator powered by IBM PureData System for Analytics N1001

The disk enclosures contain high-density, high-performance disks that are RAID protected. Each disk contains a slice of the data in the database table, along with a mirror of the data on another disk. The storage arrays are connected to the S-Blades through high-speed interconnects that allow all the disks to simultaneously stream data to the S-Blades at the fastest rate possible.

The SMP hosts are high-performance Linux servers that are set up in an active–passive configuration for high availability. The active host presents a standardized interface to external tools and applications, such as business intelligence and extract, transform, and load (ETL) tools and load utilities.

It compiles SQL queries into executable code segments called snippets, creates optimized query plans, and distributes the snippets to the S-Blades for execution. The DB2 Analytics Accelerator server also runs on the SMP host. S-Blades are intelligent processing nodes that make up the turbocharged message processing platform (MPP) engine of the appliance.

All system components are connected by means of a high-speed network fabric. PureData System for Analytics runs a customized IP-based protocol that fully uses the total cross-sectional bandwidth of the fabric and eliminates congestion even under sustained, intermittent network traffic.

The network is optimized to scale to more than a thousand nodes, while allowing each node to initiate large data transfers to every other node simultaneously. All system components are redundant.

While the hosts are active–passive, all other components in the appliance are hot-swappable. User data is fully mirrored, enabling better than 99.99 percent availability.

The PureData System for Analytics S-Blade, Based on Netezza Technology

Each S-Blade is an independent server that contains powerful multi-core CPUs, Netezza's unique multi-engine field programmable gate arrays (FPGAs), and gigabytes of RAM— all balanced and working concurrently to deliver peak performance.

FPGAs are commodity chips that are designed to process data streams at extremely fast rates. Netezza employs these chips to filter out extraneous data based on the SELECT and WHERE clauses in the SQL statement, as quickly as data can be streamed off the disk. The process of data filtering reduces the amount of data by 95 to 98 percent, freeing up downstream components from processing unnecessary amounts of data.

The S-Blades also execute an array of different database primitives such as sorts, joins, and aggregations in the CPU cores. The CPU cores are designed with ample headroom to run embedded algorithms of arbitrary complexity against large data streams for advanced analytics applications.

The S-Blade is where the key Netezza functions are performed. Each S-Blade is a combination of a standard blade server and a database accelerator card provided by Netezza. It uses IBM's "sidecar" technology to easily combine the two blades to make them act as a single logical and physical entity.

Note

The sidecar technology is commonly used by IBM to expand its blade servers to add more memory or I/O blades to each server.

Applying Data Stream Processing to DB2 Queries

A key component of Netezza's performance is the way in which its streaming architecture processes data. The Netezza architecture uniquely uses the FPGA as a turbocharger—a huge performance accelerator that allows the system not only to keep up with the data stream but also to actually accelerate the data stream through compression before processing it at line rates, ensuring no bottlenecks in the I/O path.

You can think of the way that data streaming works in Netezza as similar to an assembly line. The Netezza assembly line has various stages in the FPGA and CPU cores. Each of these stages, along with the disk and network, operate concurrently, processing different chunks of the data stream at any given point in time.

The concurrency within each data stream further increases performance relative to other architectures. Compressed data gets streamed from disk onto the assembly line at the fastest rate that the physics of the disk allows. The data could also be cached, in which case it gets served directly from memory instead of disk.

The first stage in the assembly line, the Compress Engine within the FPGA core, picks up the data block and decompresses it at wire speed, instantly transforming each block on disk into from four to eight blocks in memory. The result is a significant speedup of the slowest component in any data warehouse—the disk.

The disk block is then passed on to the Project engine or stage, which filters out columns based on parameters specified in the SELECT clause of the SQL query being processed.

The assembly line then moves the data block to the Restrict engine, which strips off rows that are not necessary to process the query, based on restrictions specified in the WHERE clause.

The Visibility engine also feeds in additional parameters to the Restrict engine, to filter out rows that should not be "seen" by a query—for example, rows belonging to a transaction that is not committed yet. The Visibility engine is critical in maintaining atomicity, consistency, isolation, and durability (ACID) compliance at streaming speeds in the Netezza unit.

The processor core picks up the uncompressed, filtered data block and performs fundamental database operations such as sorts, joins, and aggregations on it. It also applies complex algorithms that are embedded in the snippet code for advanced analytics processing. It finally assembles all the intermediate results together from the entire data stream and produces a result for the snippet. The result is then sent over the network fabric to other S-Blades or the host, as directed by the snippet code.

Comparing PureData System for Analytics Appliance Models

Figure 1.10 compares the PureData System for Analytics Appliance models. They range from a quarter rack to 10 full-rack cabinets.

IBM PureData for Analytics N1001 Appliance models

Powered by Netezza

Model	002	005	010	015	025	030	040	060	080	100
Cabinets	1/4	1/2	1	1 1/2	2	3	4	6	8	10
S-Blades	3	6	12	18	24	36	48	72	96	120
Processing Units	24	48	96	144	192	288	384	576	768	960
Capacity (TB)	8	16	32	48	64	96	128	192	256	320
Effective Capacity (TB)*	32	64	128	192	256	384	512	768	1024	1280

IBM DB2 Analytics Accelerator supports all the models

Capacity	= User data space
Effective Capacity	= User data space with compression (4x compression assumed)

Figure 1.10: IBM PureData for Analytics N1001 Appliance models

Minimizing Disk Failures

Disk failover and resiliency is highly improved. Each disk is divided into three partitions—one that holds a slice of the user's data, a mirror of data on another disk, and a temp partition that is used to hold intermediate results. All of these partitions are mirrored, including the temp partition. The primary partition is mirrored in pairs in a RAID 1 format. The temp partition is laid out across a set of eight drives in RAID 1+0 format (striped on mirrors).

Minimizing S-Blade Failures

All drives are visible to all S-Blades within a chassis. Thus, if an S-Blade fails, its drives are redistributed among the remaining online S-Blades within a chassis (each chassis has six S-Blades in it).

Summary

In this paper, we have examined how IBM DB2 Analytics Accelerator brings extremely fast performance to data-intensive and complex DB2 queries for data warehouse, business intelligence, and analytics workloads. It enables these queries to be transacted up to hundreds of times faster than was previously possible. We have covered how IBM

DB2 Analytics Accelerator makes this possible—and how the high performance and low cost of the IBM DB2 Analytics Accelerator makes it ideal for organizations to use it with data on the IBM System z platform.

In reading this paper, you have learned about the IBM DB2 Analytics Accelerator architecture and how to use the accelerator, control acceleration, and maintain its content. The paper should give you a knowledge of the new access path and which workloads and query types apply for the new access type.

For more information about the IBM DB2 Analytics Accelerator, contact your IBM sales representative or go to *http://www.ibm.com/software/data/db2/zos/analytics-accelerator*.

About the Authors

Namik Hrle works in the IBM Boeblingen Development Laboratory and is the lab's chief Information Management technologist, responsible for strategy and technology directions. As an IBM Distinguished Engineer and a member of the IBM Academy of Technology, he belongs to a small circle of the top technical leaders whose work and expertise affect the direction of IBM. He is a member of the Information Management Architecture Board, Software Group Architecture Board Steering Committee, Technical Experts Council, and many other IBM expert teams that work on strategic technology topics as well as address customers' information technology needs and requirements. He is the holder of numerous patents, outstanding technical achievements, and author recognition and corporate awards.

Ruiping Li is a Senior Engineer in DB2 for z/OS development at IBM Silicon Valley Lab. She is the technical lead responsible for the DB2 query acceleration support for the IBM DB2 Analytics Accelerator. She has been the development lead for DB2 9 for z/OS new feature optimistic locking support and DB2 10 for z/OS new feature timestamp with time zone data type support and has also been the key developer for some other important functionality. This functionality includes pureXML index exploitation, complex queries, MQTs, and multiple CCSID features in DB2 for z/OS.

Wolfgang Hengstler has held positions within IBM for more than 30 years—first in software development and then in product and market management for IBM Software Group, IBM Storage and Technology Group, IBM Tivoli, and IBM Global Services. Wolfgang's projects have involved operating system components, OO wrapping technology, system automation products, and hosting services. He currently works in the IBM Information Management development lab in Boeblingen, Germany, and is part of a global product management team focusing on data warehousing on IBM System z.

Acknowledgements

Thanks to the following people for their invaluable contributions to this paper and for making it possible:

- *Surekha Parekh, Worldwide Marketing Program Director, IBM DB2 for z/OS, United Kingdom*
- *Guogen Zhang, Former IBM Distinguished Engineer, Silicon Valley Lab*

DB2 10 for z/OS
Query Optimization Update

by Terry Purcell
IBM Silicon Valley Lab

IBM DB2 for z/OS customers expect improved performance in each release while maintaining the stability and reliability to which they have grown accustomed from the mainframe environment. DB2 10 for z/OS continues this theme, with significant attention given to improved plan management, runtime optimizations, and new access path choices.

The DB2 optimizer goal is to provide continual improvement in performance for new and existing workloads while maintaining the stability and reliability of the access path choices on which our customers rely for their traditional workloads. Optimizer theorists and academics will point out the challenges for any query optimizer to guarantee perfection in access path selection. But the reality is, our DB2 for z/OS customers don't want excuses; they need solutions that deliver this reliability in performance without increasing cost.

So, how is IBM addressing these challenges? What you will see are the following major themes for enhancements to the DB2 10 for z/OS optimizer:

- ✓ Predicate processing improvements regardless of access path
- ✓ New access path choices to improve common query patterns
- ✓ Enhancements to plan management

Predicate processing improvements are just that: more efficient predicate evaluation to reduce CPU consumption. New access path choices provide opportunities for improved performance for query patterns that have been identified as important to our DB2 customers. And, finally, plan management provides the capability to recover a prior static package upon access path regression. Also new in DB2 10 for z/OS is the ability to reuse the prior access path for BIND/REBIND.

This three-pronged approach to enhancing query performance is anticipated to provide a more positive customer experience for the performance of your workloads than any release in recent memory. This is also likely to serve as the model for future DB2 releases to provide improved performance with reduced exposure to regression risk.

Access Path Management

The reason customers historically embraced static SQL over dynamic is that static provides a degree of certainty and stability, as its dictionary definition clearly states: Static "shows little or no change," while dynamic implies ever-changing.

Just because an SQL application is dynamic in nature does not mean the DB2 optimizer will have a problem in its access path selection. However, there is a benefit to leaving the access path alone if it is already performing well. And you have greater control over this for static SQL than dynamic. Stability is only one consideration; the other is avoiding the overhead of BIND/PREPARE if there is no desire to explore a new access path.

The topic of access path management encompasses both reducing dynamic PREPARE overhead (by avoiding PREPARE where possible) and addressing the potential instability that can occur from large-scale BINDs or REBINDs.

Dynamic statement cache enhancements

In a dynamic SQL environment, minimizing the overhead of PREPARE by exploiting the dynamic statement cache is one goal. The dynamic statement cache allows subsequent executions of the same SQL statement to reuse the previously PREPAREd access path, rather than preparing the statement again for every execution.

For effective reuse of a prior execution, the statement must match between executions. This is why we encourage SQL applications to be coded using parameter markers, rather than literal values. Applications that have not been coded to use parameter markers will require a new PREPARE for each execution unless a recent execution of the same statement has occurred with exactly the same literal values. This is often unlikely.

Literal replacement

DB2 10 for z/OS introduces the capability to replace the literals with a marker so that queries containing literals can now be reused in the cache. The literals will be replaced with an ampersand (@), which is similar to, but not the same as, a parameter marker. This feature is referred to as *literal replacement* or *literal concentration*. The idea is that you concentrate all the various literal values into a single common ampersand for each predicate. Repeat executions of the same query can subsequently benefit from a previously cached copy of the query in the dynamic statement, rather than issuing a new PREPARE.

To enable literal concentration, perform one of the following steps:

- On the client, code the PREPARE ATTRIBUTES clause to include the CONCENTRATE STATEMENTS WITH LITERALS option.
- On the client side, change the JCC driver to include the keyword enableliteralReplacement='YES'.
- In the Open Database Connectivity (ODBC) initialization file in z/OS, set the LITERALREPLACEMENT keyword. This option enables literal replacement for all SQL coming into DB2 through ODBC.

The lookup sequence for the SQL execution is to first look up the cache for the SQL with literals to see whether a prior copy has been cached with the same literals. If such a copy is found, the PREPARE is avoided and the prior access path used.

Otherwise, the literals are replaced with an ampersand and the lookup is repeated. If a match is found, the matched access path is reused. Otherwise, a new PREPARE is issued and the resultant query and access path are stored in the dynamic statement cache.

For transactional workloads with repeated, short-running queries, there is significant benefit in avoiding the overhead of PREPARE for each execution of the query. While replacing a literal with an ampersand or coding a parameter marker can result in reduced PREPARE overhead, it also means the optimizer cannot take advantage of the literal values to improve its access path decision using FREQVAL or HISTOGRAM statistics.

For example, if statistics show that STATUS='Y' is 99 percent of the data and STATUS='N' is 1 percent, a query with WHERE STATUS='N' will recognize that an index may be a good choice for the access path. However, WHERE STATUS='Y' would be best served with a table space scan. Replacing the literal with an ampersand means WHERE STATUS=& cannot take advantage of the frequency statistics.

Provided an efficient access path is chosen for transactional queries, reducing PREPARE overhead should be the goal. Therefore, this is a tradeoff that most DBAs are willing to accept because PREPARE overhead can be easily observed.

Parameter markers will still provide better performance than the literal replacement technique due to literal replacement potentially requiring an additional cache lookup. Additional storage is also needed for original predicate attributes such as data type and length with literal replacement.

Regardless of whether coding parameter markers may be more efficient than literal replacement, the key point is that this enhancement is focused on applications that cannot or did not use parameter markers. Therefore, for transactional workloads, the literal replacement technique is likely to be more efficient than issuing a PREPARE—assuming no access path regressions result from hiding the literal values from the optimizer. Transactional workloads generally are made up of many repeated executions of the same query.

In reporting, ad hoc, or query workloads, it is preferable to let the optimizer see the literal values for improved access path selection. For such queries, the PREPARE overhead is a small percentage of the overall query cost. Thus, the focus is on giving the optimizer sufficient information to determine an efficient access path choice rather than shortcutting PREPARE. In general, these workloads do not repeat executions of the same query patterns, so there is minimal benefit to avoiding PREPARE.

For workloads that need both reduced PREPARE overhead and improved information for the optimizer, consider using the REOPT(ONCE) BIND option in conjunction with literal replacement. The optimizer will use the set of literals from the first execution of the query for its access path determination. This option is a good choice if the query consistently looks for the same values/ranges for the skewed or range predicates. However, it may not result in the best performance if, for example, the query flips from STATUS='Y' to 'N', because the access path determination will be based on the first execution.

The target for this enhancement is applications that cannot or have not used parameter markers. Therefore, if a query currently contains a mixture of parameter markers and literal values, it will not be eligible for literal replacement—because the application can obviously tolerate parameter markers.

When the query contains a mixture, the assumption is that there is an intention to code parameter markers for predicates that change frequently but whose change will not impact the access path, and to code literals for those for which the optimizer would benefit from seeing the literal.

Consider this example:

WHERE ACCOUNT_NUMBER = ? AND STATUS = 'Y'

There may be millions of distinct ACCOUNT_NUMBERs, and each execution of the query uses a different value, which means the predicate is a good candidate for a parameter marker. The STATUS='Y' predicate may have two possible values and is likely to be skewed. Therefore, this predicate is a good candidate for a literal value. A query coded this way would not be a candidate for literal replacement because of the mix of parameter markers and literals.

Limitations exist for literal replacements, including lack of support for LIKE predicates. Also, the SQL text replaced with ampersands is not considered valid external syntax; it is an internal representation only. Therefore, externalized copies of the SQL with literals replaced cannot be fed into EXPLAIN or used for statement-level optimization hints or options (which are new to DB2 10).

Access plan stability or plan management

DB2 9 for z/OS delivered *plan management*, which supports a backup and recovery capability for the access plans of statically bound packages. DB2 10 for z/OS provides some incremental enhancements to the original plan management usability while also introducing some quantum leaps forward in reducing the impact of access path regression for static SQL.

It should be noted that one of the most common comments or questions related to the DB2 9 enhancement is regarding the name—"plan management"—because it applies only to static packages. In query optimization, "plan" refers to the access plan or access path. Optimizer Development therefore uses the term "plan management" to refer, not to a plan or a package, but to the access plan chosen by the optimizer.

Given that DB2 9 has been generally available for more than five years, the retort to this question about the name plan management has improved. To this date, there is no good answer as to why no similar questions arise about the PLAN_TABLE.

The success of plan management in DB2 9 for z/OS has resulted in the first enhancement seen in DB2 10: a simple change of the default value for the PLANMGMT ZPARM from OFF in DB2 9 to ENABLED in DB2 10. We want you to exploit this backup and recovery capability as an insurance policy for your access paths. Query performance has become mission critical for many of our customers, who cannot tolerate performance regressions because of either service level agreements or the high utilization rates for their mainframe applications.

ZPARM PLANMGMT (and associated BIND option) controls only the capability for backup/recovery (REBIND SWITCH) of static packages. The new DB2 10 for z/OS plan management and EXPLAIN functions do not require this parameter to be enabled; however, I will repeat the recommendation to enable PLANMGMT as per the DB2 10 default.

A new catalog table, SYSIBM.SYSPACKCOPY, has been added to hold the metadata for the previous and original copies, which was previously available only in the SYSPACKAGE catalog table. To see information in DB2 9 for the previous/original copies, the user had to REBIND(SWITCH) that copy to become the current one and thus populate SYSPACKAGE. This step was inconvenient if you only needed to view this detail for the saved copies. In DB2 10 for z/OS, SYSPACKCOPY is populated during the Enable New Function Mode (ENFM) process.

Space usage in SPT01 was one concern for DB2 9 customers due to the 64 GB data set limit for SPT01. DB2 for z/OS Version 8 and DB2 9 for z/OS supported compression of SPT01. Several solutions exist to reduce SPT01 space consumption and avoid the 64 GB limit in DB2 10.

First, SPT01 becomes a partition by growth (PBG) table space, and, with APAR PM27811, the use of inline large objects (LOBs) enables the compression of SPT01.

An additional enhancement is the APRETAINDUP REBIND (and REBIND TRIGGER) package option. This option specifies whether an access plan is saved as either an original or a previous copy if the newly generated plan is equivalent. The default is YES—to retain the duplicates. Arguably, use of APRETAINDUP(NO) would result in space savings when using plan management basic or extended (the DB2 10 for z/OS default) because duplicate access plans are not saved.

When using APRETAINDUP(NO) in DB2 10 for z/OS, the existing (current) plan that is being replaced must have been bound in V9 or V10 for the access plan comparison to occur.

That concludes the incremental enhancements to the backup and recovery capability of plan management in DB2 10 for z/OS.

DB2 10 Takes Plan Management to the Next Level

The backup and recovery capability of the DB2 9 for z/OS plan management was a very welcome addition to REBIND. However, DB2 10 for z/OS brings significantly more value to reduce the risk of access path regression across REBIND. In DB2 9, a new BIND/REBIND causes a compressed copy of the PLAN_TABLE rows for each SQL statement in the package to be saved in the directory/SPT01. The internal representation of the PLAN_TABLE, which DB2 Development refers to as the *Explain Data Block (EDB)*, is used as the basis for numerous enhancements to plan management—which will be outlined in the upcoming section. What this means, however, is that many of these enhancements are available only for BINDs/REBINDs that have occurred in DB2 9 or later.

Many customers associate the recommendation to REBIND as a way to expose their queries to the improvements in the optimizer. But there are many situations in which customers may not be ready to expose themselves to access path changes but where REBIND is recommended or forced.

Across a DB2 release, REBIND is recommended to take advantage of the new release runtime structures. While prior release runtime structures are tolerated in the new release (this is true for runtime structures from DB2 V6 and later in DB2 10), optimizations such as SPROCs are disabled. However, during a migration, it is reasonable to assume that system stability is desired from the migration before exposing the application to access path changes, due to concerns about regression.

There is another, often less-discussed reason for REBINDing in each new release, and that is that older runtime structures are at greater risk of instability from either an abend or incorrect output. DB2 tolerates prior-release runtime structures from V6 onward in DB2 10, but there is still the question as to whether DB2 was able to test your V6 or V7 runtime structure in DB2 10 testing. Considering the number of possible access paths, and the specific maintenance level when the package was bound, it is difficult to imagine that every combination received test coverage. The bottom line is that it is safer to be more current than two or more releases prior with your REBINDs.

Given that DB2 Development are encouraging a REBIND at least once per release, it is important that we are also able to address the main reason why customers avoid REBIND—which is generally because of the risk of regression. For this reason, DB2 10 adds a new parameter for BIND and REBIND that provides the capability to control when a new access path is considered for these commands. APREUSE (Access Path Reuse) will attempt to BIND/REBIND using the prior access path as an internal hint to drive the new access path choice. The supported parameter values are NO/NONE (default and standard BIND/REBIND behavior) or ERROR, whereby the BIND/REBIND will try to reuse the prior access path; if the prior access path cannot be reused, an error will be issued and the BIND/REBIND will fail. The level of granularity is on the package, which means a failure of any single SQL to reuse the prior access path will cause all SQL statements in the package to fail in their reuse.

Another way of looking at APREUSE is that DB2 10 for z/OS gives you greater control over when you want to expose your application to new access path choices. Rather than being forced to open up new access path choices when REBIND is recommended across migration, when APAR ++HOLD information recommends REBIND, or when a schema change invalidates the package, APREUSE lets you differentiate REBIND (and BIND) when you do and do not want to expose your application to new access path choices. This capability is a significant leap forward in providing further stabilization and avoidance of regression for static SQL.

A second additional BIND/REBIND parameter choice, APCOMPARE, performs an access path comparison between the prior access path and the newly generated access path. The options are NO/NONE (default and no comparison performed), WARN (warning messages are written to the PLAN_TABLE.REMARKS column to identify access path differences), and ERROR (any access path difference results in failure of the BIND/REBIND). Arguably, APCOMPARE(WARN) should be the default for customers performing a BIND or REBIND of their static packages, because this setting simply externalizes meaningful information to the PLAN_TABLE about changes in the access path. APCOMPARE(ERROR) may be less useful, as it allows a BIND/REBIND to seek a new access path choice, but, due to the ERROR option, the BIND/REBIND will fail if a new access path is chosen.

To clarify both APREUSE and APCOMPARE, APREUSE asks BIND/REBIND to attempt to reuse the prior access path. APCOMPARE, without APREUSE, will allow a new access path choice (same as BIND/REBIND prior to APREUSE) but will issue PLAN_TABLE messages to identify changes in the access path.

Note
APREUSE or APCOMPARE are valid only for packages bound in DB2 9 for z/OS or later. Any usage of APREUSE/APCOMPARE on a pre-DB2 9 package will be unable to internally use the EDB for reuse or comparison. However, this will not fail the package, which may be misleading to some users.

EXPLAIN enhancements

The theme of plan management is not complete without discussing the externalization of the access path in the PLAN_TABLE and other extended explain tables.

It has been a longstanding requirement from our customers to be able to explain the existing access path for a previously bound package. This capability is necessary for cases where the prior BIND/REBIND used EXPLAIN(NO), or when the PLAN_TABLE rows are no longer in existence. Issuing a new EXPLAIN will potentially produce a new access path and thus not represent what is currently executing.

Therefore, the requirement is to "tell me what I have." I'll discuss the DB2 solution next, and also a solution for the requirement to "tell me what I would get if I performed a BIND/REBIND today."

DB2 10 for z/OS adds a new option to EXPLAIN—EXPLAIN PACKAGE—for the requirement to "tell me what I have." This option allows extraction of the existing access path from the package EDB. The output from EXPLAIN PACKAGE is inserted into the PLAN_TABLE. No other extended explain tables are populated by EXPLAIN PACKAGE. And it is possible to specify the COPY as the current, previous, or original to extract— as can be seen in the syntax diagram in Figure 2.1.

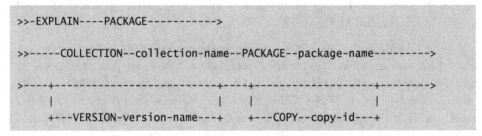

Figure 2.1: EXPLAIN PACKAGE syntax diagram

In this scenario, the term "EXPLAIN" is really a misnomer; this is actually an "EXTRACT." An EXPLAIN has historically implied the generation of a new access path choice. However, instead of introducing a new "EXTRACT" keyword, DB2 has piggy-backed on the EXPLAIN statement for this enhancement. As with many of the DB2 10 plan management enhancements that rely on the internal representation of the access path from the EDB, this enhancement is supported *only* if the package is from DB2 9 or later.

For those who want to ask the question, "What would the new access path be if I performed a BIND/REBIND today?" there is a new EXPLAIN(ONLY) option for BIND/ REBIND. EXPLAIN has always had the options YES/NO, and the addition of ONLY lets this "What if?" question be answered easily without impacting the existing package. Custom-ers may have accomplished this previously by performing a BIND to a dummy collection or by manually explaining the SQL outside the package.

It should be noted that extracting the SQL outside the package and issuing an EXPLAIN may not always be equivalent—as this would become a dynamic EXPLAIN rather than a static EXPLAIN. A dynamic EXPLAIN will not consider indexes in a restricted state, whereas a static EXPLAIN will. Also, data type or length differences between the host variable and predicate column are masked if you perform a dynamic EXPLAIN—and, despite the fact that DB2 V8 improved indexability for mismatched data type/length predicates, some behavioral differences still exist.

For EXPLAIN(ONLY), the BIND/REBIND is performed, the chosen access path is written out to the PLAN_TABLE, and, finally, the BIND/REBIND is rolled back. The PLAN_ TABLE entries remain and are flagged with 'Y' in the new BIND_EXPLAIN_ONLY column so that customers can determine that these PLAN_TABLE rows—despite the fact that they are associated with packages—came from a BIND/REBIND with EXPLAIN(ONLY) and may not correlate to any current access path in the catalog. Locking/concurrency require-ments are the same with EXPLAIN(ONLY) as for a standard BIND/REBIND.

An additional parameter is available to have BIND/REBIND perform a syntax check as well without creating the actual package. You can use this option, SQLERROR(CHECK), independently of EXPLAIN(ONLY). The SQLERROR(CHECK) parameter of the BIND/REBIND commands was targeted specifically to those customers who may have their development and test systems on another DB2 platform, and whose only opportunity to validate the package is in their production DB2 for z/OS system.

With all these new additions to EXPLAIN, it becomes a challenge for users to understand the usage scenario for each EXPLAIN option. Therefore, it is important to summarize the various EXPLAIN usages to help clarify their function.

As Figure 2.2 outlines, the following summarizes the key usages of EXPLAIN:

- BIND/REBIND with EXPLAIN(YES) is an existing choice and performs the following:

  ○ Generates a new access path (or attempts to reuse prior if APREUSE(ERROR))
  ○ Populates the PLAN_TABLE
  ○ Creates a new copy of the package

- BIND/REBIND with EXPLAIN(ONLY) is a new choice and performs the following:

  ○ Generates a new access path (or attempts to reuse prior if APREUSE(ERROR))
  ○ Populates the PLAN_TABLE
  ○ Does *not* create a new copy of the package

- EXPLAIN PLAN is an existing choice executed from SPUFI/QMF/DSNTEP2 and so on and performs the following:

  ○ Generates a new access path
  ○ Populates the PLAN_TABLE

- EXPLAIN PACKAGE is a new choice and performs the following:

  ○ Does *not* generate a new access path; extracts the existing access path from the package
  ○ Populates the PLAN_TABLE

- EXPLAIN STMTCACHE STMTID|STMTOKEN is an existing choice and performs the following:

  ○ Does *not* generate a new access path; extracts the existing access path
  ○ Populates the PLAN_TABLE

---

*Options in **bold** are new to DB2 10.*

BIND/REBIND with EXPLAIN(YES)
Generates a new access path, populates PLAN_TABLE, and creates a new package

BIND/REBIND with EXPLAIN(**ONLY**)
Generates a new access path, populates PLAN_TABLE, but **does *not* create a new package**

EXPLAIN PLAN (issued in SPUFI/QMF/DSNTEP2, etc.)
Generates a new access path and populates PLAN_TABLE

EXPLAIN **PACKAGE**
Does not generate new access path; **extracts existing access path** from package and populates PLAN_TABLE

EXPLAIN STMTCACHE STMTID|STMTOKEN
Does not generate new access path; extracts existing and populates PLAN_TABLE

Figure 2.2: EXPLAIN usage scenarios

Instance-based statement hints

Optimization Hints (opthints for short), first delivered in DB2 V6, have been embraced by some customers as a way to override a problem access path choice or stabilize queries to avoid access path change. It is also fair to say that opthints have been avoided by many other customers due to their cumbersome nature or the challenges for customers to micromanage access paths. The previously discussed DB2 10 for z/OS plan management enhancements may reduce the need for hints to be used to stabilize an access path.

In addition to the plan management enhancements, DB2 10 improves the infrastructure and usability of opthints, so that customers continue to have a way to override an inefficient access path choice if other more suitable solutions aren't viable.

The first enhancement related to opthints introduces a catalog infrastructure to support a more general form of hints. This is referred to as the *access path repository*, which holds important query metadata (such as query text), query access paths, and other information, such as optimization options.

The repository consists of several new catalog tables:

*   SYSIBM.SYSQUERY is the central table of the access path repository. It holds one row for each static or dynamic SQL query that is to exploit user-specified hints or options.
*   SYSIBM.SYSQUERYPLAN holds the plan hint information (if hints are specified) for each query in the SYSIBM.SYSQUERY table.

- SYSIBM.SYSQUERYOPTS holds the option information (if options are specified) for each query in SYSIBM.SYSQUERY.

The original opthints delivered in DB2 V6 have often presented challenges for customers to maintain, and one reason for this is because they are tied to a query number. For static SQL, this means that if the application programmer adds or removes lines of code, the precompiler will generate a new query number for each SQL statement occurring after the code change. DB2 V6 also provided the QUERYNO clause, which could be added to an SQL statement to ensure that the same query number was used across application changes. For dynamic SQL, this was the required way to match a statement to a hint. For both static and dynamic, however, altering the SQL is often impractical and thus was rarely adopted as a solution.

DB2 10 adds an alternative way to associate a statement and a hint—using the query text. Similar to the concept of a dynamic statement cache text match, the SQL text is tied to the hint such that a static BIND or dynamic PREPARE will attempt to look up the statement text to find a matching hint. A hint can therefore be created irrespective of its usage for dynamic or static SQL—and thus the hint can be given a global scope or a package-level scope.

The hints are stored in the access path repository. The PLAN_TABLE isn't going away, however. Instead, there is now an alternate method for looking up the hint that makes it simpler for dynamic and more stable for application changes in static SQL.

While tying the hint to the statement text means changes in query numbers will not affect the hint, changes to the SQL statement will result in the match failing.

To take advantage of the new hints process, take the following steps:

1. Enable the OPTHINTS ZPARM.
2. Populate the user table DSN_USERQUERY_TABLE with the query text.

   ◦ Insert from SYSPACKSTMT (static) or DSN_STATEMENT_CACHE_TABLE (dynamic) to ensure that the correct DB2 representation of the SQL text is used.

3. Populate PLAN_TABLE with the corresponding hints.

   ◦ *Note:* Choose any arbitrary QUERYNO. The QUERYNO value must match between PLAN_TABLE and DSN_USERQUERY_TABLE. Duplicate query numbers in the PLAN_TABLE may result in difficulty matching the PLAN_TABLE and DSN_USERQUERY_TABLE rows.

4. Execute the new command BIND QUERY to integrate the hint into the repository.
5. The next package BIND/REBIND or dynamic PREPARE can pick up the hint.

To remove the query from the repository, use the FREE QUERY command.

Instance-based (or statement-level) options

The same infrastructure that allows an access path hint to be matched to the statement text is also extended to allow statement-level scope for a small number of BIND parameters and ZPARMs, namely:

- REOPT
- STARJOIN enablement and number of tables qualified for STARJOIN
- Parallelism enablement and number of degrees

This has been another longstanding customer requirement to provide improved granularity for the REOPT BIND option. Once a query is identified that would benefit from REOPT(ALWAYS), it is common for the customer to not want the overhead of REOPT for all other statements in the package. The previous recommendation has been to separate out the targeted query into a separate package, which is often impractical.

The steps to implement these statement-level options are similar to those for statement-level hints—minus the PLAN_TABLE input:

1. Enable the OPTHINTS ZPARM.
2. Populate the user table DSN_USERQUERY_TABLE with the query text.

   - Insert from SYSPACKSTMT (static) or DSN_STATEMENT_CACHE_TABLE (dynamic) to ensure that the correct DB2 representation of the SQL text is used.
   - *Note*: Choose any arbitrary QUERYNO value that does *not* currently exist in the PLAN_TABLE. The reason is that BIND QUERY first looks to find the PLAN_TABLE rows; if not found, it then looks at the options in DSN_USERQUERY_TABLE.

3. Execute the new command BIND QUERY to integrate the statement-level options into the repository.
4. The next package BIND/REBIND or dynamic PREPARE can pick up the new options.

Hints and options are mutually exclusive. Therefore, at this stage it is only possible to have either a hint or options for a given statement in SYSQUERY.

Predicate Processing and Runtime Optimizations

The most welcome performance improvements for customers are those that require minimal action or intervention. And the performance enhancements in DB2 10 for z/OS include predicate processing improvements and runtime optimizations that can be exploited within existing access path choices, as well as those that offer new choices to the DB2 for z/OS optimizer.

It is well understood by DB2 Development that customers are continually pushed to do more with less—whether that is individual DBAs having to manage more DB2 subsystems or the systems themselves increasing data volumes and throughput without a corresponding increase in available capacity. Thus, improving performance is among the highest priorities for DB2 Development.

Improvements to predicate application for IN and OR predicates

DB2 10 for z/OS delivers several enhancements to IN-list and OR predicate processing.

The first enhancement involves an improvement to the execution performance of long IN-lists and complex AND/OR predicates that are chosen as index screening or stage 1. The improvement comes from DB2 being able to exit the predicate application process as soon as a true or false condition is triggered that allows further processing to be avoided. While DB2 has always been able to stop processing once a row is qualified or disqualified (depending on the predicate context), DB2 10 for z/OS delivers additional optimizations to traversing the predicate tree.

Unfortunately, there is no way to identify a query as a candidate for this optimization—which raises the question, "Why is there any detail at all here about this enhancement?" The answer is because of customer questions as to why they have seen some queries achieve CPU reductions without an access path change. One possible explanation is of the aforementioned enhancement.

The next enhancement relates to IN-list predicates that are candidates for index matching. When IN-list predicates are filtering, matching index access is often desirable using these IN-list predicates. Before DB2 10, DB2 could match on the first IN-list (based on the index key column order) and continue matching on available predicates until a second IN-list was encountered.

Basically, DB2 could only match on one IN-list, and any subsequent IN-list predicates would be applied as index screening. In situations where the second IN-list was more filtering, performance was not always optimal.

Similarly, when choosing matching IN-list access, DB2 would not choose list prefetch, which is preferred if the index has a poor cluster ratio. Instead, DB2 might choose to match on one less column (without the IN-list) so that list prefetch could be exploited. Thus, DB2 would trade improved data I/O performance for less index matching and instead apply the IN-list as screening.

DB2 10 for z/OS addresses these issues with IN-list predicates by allowing the optimizer to consider converting the IN-list to a table such that the IN-list processing performs more like a join. This allows matching on multiple IN-lists and also list prefetch to be supported.

However, this IN-list table will be chosen only if matching on multiple IN-lists is chosen, or if list prefetch is chosen with matching IN-list access. Otherwise, the previous type of IN-list matching is considered (ACCESSTYPE='N').

In the EXPLAIN output in the PLAN_TABLE, this access to the in-memory table is associated with a new table type, 'I', and a new access type, 'IN'. Figure 2.3 shows the PLAN_TABLE output for IN-list table access with list prefetch.

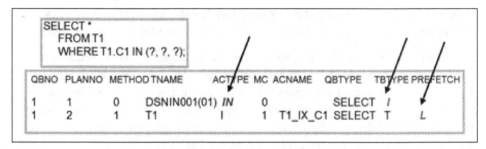

Figure 2.3: IN-list table example with list prefetch

It should be noted that list prefetch will execute once per IN-list element. It is *not* a consolidated list prefetch access for all elements. Therefore, if the IN-list elements are each of a high cardinality, there may be no benefit to choosing list prefetch.

Another enhancement to IN-list predicate processing is *transitive closure* support for IN-lists. The U.S. National Institute of Standards and Technology (NIST) defines transitive closure as: "An extension or superset of a binary relation such that whenever *(a,b)* and *(b,c)* are in the extension, *(a,c)* is also in the extension." To put that into a query predicate perspective, if *A=B* and *A=1*, then *B* also *=1*. DB2 has supported transitive closure for =, <, <=, >, >=, and BETWEEN for many releases, but DB2 10 for z/OS adds support for IN-lists.

Figure 2.4 shows an example where IN-list predicate transitive closure (PTC) is now possible.

```
SELECT *
FROM T1, T2
WHERE T1.C1 = T2.C1
  AND T1.C1 IN (?, ?, ?)

  AND T2.C1 IN (?, ?, ?)   <--optimizer can generate
                             this predicate via PTC
```

Figure 2.4: IN-list Predicate Transitive Closure (PTC) example

Without PTC, DB2 is likely to choose T1 as the leading table in the join sequence because there is only filtering on T1. By generating an additional predicate, AND T2.C1 IN (?, ?, ?), DB2 may consider the alternate join sequence with T2 as the first (outer) table in the join sequence. This gives DB2 greater opportunity to choose the most efficient access path, regardless of how the query is coded.

OR predicate processing improvements: Online cursor scrolling

We have discussed some enhancements to predicate processing for IN and OR predicates and the improved index matching capabilities for IN-lists. In prior releases of DB2, there has always been a link between OR and IN predicates, with DB2 rewriting simple OR conditions against the same column to become IN-lists. A simple example is WHERE C1 = 1 OR C1 = 2, which DB2 rewrites to become WHERE C1 IN (1,2). This behavior has not changed in DB2 10 for z/OS.

The DB2 10 enhancements target more complex OR predicates that are not candidates for this simple rewrite to IN-lists. To improve processing for OR predicates, DB2 introduces a new access type: *range-list access*. Range-list access refers to a "list of ranges" separated by OR. This is similar to IN-list access in its processing, but without representing the more-complex OR conditions as a simplified IN-list predicate.

The two original targets for range-list access are:

- *Scrolling/paging SQL:* Common in CICS and other online web applications where the application wants to fetch the next *n* rows to fill a screen. This is not to be confused with scrollable cursors, which require the application to keep the transaction open for scrolling forward/backward through the result.
- *Complex* OR *predicates against the same columns:* Where the OR predicates are not simple equal predicates that DB2 would convert to an IN, but may include range predicates and/or compound predicates within each OR. The construct is common in some ERP applications that write predicates in disjunctive normal form.

For both query patterns, the following conditions must be true to support range-list access:

- The OR predicate must refer to a single table.
- Each OR predicate can be mapped to the same index.
- Each OR has at least one matching predicate, given the chosen index.

In this section, we discuss the (online) scrolling query pattern. Consider the example shown in Figure 2.5.

```
WHERE (LASTNAME='JONES' AND FIRSTNAME>'WENDY')
   OR (LASTNAME>'JONES')
ORDER BY LASTNAME, FIRSTNAME;
```

Figure 2.5: Cursor scrolling example as a range-list candidate

This range-list example demonstrates scrolling through the phone book with current cursor position at "JONES, WENDY". To scroll forward from this position, the user may code the WHERE clause predicates as shown in the figure. The first OR condition (LASTNAME='JONES' AND FIRSTNAME>'WENDY') requests the remaining "JONES" after the current position. The second OR condition (LASTNAME>'JONES') requests the rows for the subsequent last names after "JONES".

The new access method can convert this OR predicate into a range-list with two ranges (one range for each OR). Therefore, there will be at most two index probes given the PHONEBOOK index on LASTNAME, FIRSTNAME. The first probe is for LASTNAME='JONES' and FIRSTNAME>'WENDY'. And once FETCHing exhausts all qualified rows from the first probe, the second probe will be issued for LASTNAME >'JONES'. These rows appear in the index in ascending order, which satisfies the ORDER BY, and thus there is no requirement to sort the rows.

Prior to DB2 10, matching index access for this example required multi-index access, list prefetch, and a final sort to satisfy the ORDER BY. For this reason, it was common for users to code a redundant predicate, AND LASTNAME >= 'JONES', to support single-matching index access. Figure 2.6 shows this approach.

```
WHERE ((LASTNAME='JONES' AND FIRSTNAME>'WENDY')
   OR (LASTNAME>'JONES'))
AND (LASTNAME >= 'JONES')
ORDER BY LASTNAME, FIRSTNAME;
```

Figure 2.6: Scrolling example with redundant predicate for matching index access

In this code, with the added (redundant) predicate AND (LASTNAME >= 'JONES'), DB2 was able to choose single-matching index access, although prior to DB2 10, the best DB2 could do was match on one column using this redundant predicate. And the original predicates were applied as index screening—which means DB2 would position in the index as matching on LASTNAME='JONES' and then have to scan through all FIRSTNAMEs from "A" to "W" to reach FIRSTNAME>'WENDY' using the pre-DB2 10 approach. With range-list access, DB2 can use both predicates on LASTNAME and FIRSTNAME to start the initial position in the index at JONES, WENDY.

In DB2 10, the optimizer may choose range-list or any existing access method, including multi-index access. It is important to note that the optimizer will make a cost-based decision. One factor that is often unknown to the optimizer is whether the application will FETCH 10 or 20 rows and close the cursor—unless the query has OPTIMIZE FOR n ROWS coded (or FETCH FIRST n ROWS ONLY). Therefore, it is not guaranteed that range-list will be chosen for this query pattern.

There is a second use case that also fits this scrolling type pattern but is unrelated to online applications, and that is batch restart logic. Range-list access is targeted more toward the online scrolling pattern, rather than batch restart usage, which is one reason why DB2 is not more aggressive when choosing range-list, since DB2 does not know whether the same pattern is for an online or a batch application. As mentioned, the OPTIMIZE FOR or FETCH FIRST clause is the best way to indicate to DB2 that this is an online query that is requesting a subset of the qualified rows.

OR predicate processing improvements: Other range-list usages

Range-list applies not only to the scrolling type SQL but to any complex OR conditions that can map to a single index. In Figure 2.7, range-list can be chosen with each OR leg having two matching columns on the index on LASTNAME, FIRSTNAME. Range-list would also be applicable if the index were on FIRSTNAME, LASTNAME, or only on LASTNAME, or only on FIRSTNAME. As mentioned, one requirement for consideration of range-list access is that each OR leg must support matching index access for the same index.

```
WHERE (LASTNAME='JONES' AND FIRSTNAME='WENDY')
   OR (LASTNAME='SMITH' AND FIRSTNAME='JOHN');
```

Figure 2.7: Non-scrolling range-list candidate

Prior to DB2 10, the optimizer could choose only multi-index access for matching index access due to the OR conditions. In DB2 10, the optimizer can choose either range-list or multi-index access based on cost. Because range-list does not support list prefetch, but multi-index access requires list prefetch, it is expected to see range-list chosen for this type of SQL with a high cluster ratio index or if very few rows qualify, and multi-index access chosen for lower cluster ratio indexes.

Range-list EXPLAIN representation

The PLAN_TABLE representation for range-list includes a new access type: ACCESSTYPE='NR'. One row will appear for each OR condition, since each OR may have a different number of MATCHCOLS. Column MIXOPSEQ (multi-index operation sequence) provides an ordering of the range-list rows.

Figure 2.8 borrows the range-list example from Figure 2.5 and reverses the order of the WHERE clause predicates to highlight an interesting nuance of the EXPLAIN output. The simplified EXPLAIN output shows the single predicate (LASTNAME > 'JONES') with MATCHCOLS=1 listed first in the PLAN_TABLE followed by the MATCHCOLS=2 predicates. This PLAN_TABLE output matches the coding sequence, and, in this example, does

```
WHERE (LASTNAME> 'JONES')
   OR (LASTNAME= 'JONES' AND FIRSTNAME> 'WENDY')
ORDER BY LASTNAME, FIRSTNAME;
```

QBlockno	Planno	Accessname	Access_Type	Matchcols	Mixopseq
1	1	IX1	NR	1	1
1	1	IX1	NR	2	2

New access type (NR = IN-List Range)   Coding seq

Figure 2.8: Range-list EXPLAIN representation

not represent the order in which the values associated with those predicates would appear in the index.

Range-list, if chosen, will access the index in the sequence that allows a sort to be avoided (if ORDER BY or GROUP BY is coded). The PLAN_TABLE is populated at BIND/ PREPARE, and for queries with host variables or parameter markers, it is not known what literal values will be used in the query.

The DB2 implementation of range-list will re-order the OR conditions at runtime based on the literal values. Thus, it is not possible for BIND/PREPARE to know the order in which these conditions will be executed.

Customers might ask the question, "But for the 'screen-scrolling SQL'—such as the example in Figure 2.8—you know the order of the execution even with host variables, as it is most MATCHCOLS to least MATCHCOLS. Why don't you order the PLAN_TABLE rows to reflect this?"

First, this question takes a very narrow view of the range-list enhancement. As outlined, the enhancement covers more than the screen-scrolling scenario. But more important, because DB2 implemented the ordering of execution of the OR predicates at runtime (execution time), BIND/PREPARE is not aware of the ordering. And enhancing DB2 to also provide recognition of the likely order at BIND/PREPARE is of minimal value.

The reason is because it is not a guarantee without knowing the literal values—and most SQLs use parameter markers or host variables. DB2 will always order the OR predicates based on the literal values used to support moving through the index in the direction to support ORDER BY/GROUP BY ordering, or in ascending sequence if no particular order is required.

Therefore, for effective access path analysis, all that is important to understand is that ACCESSTYPE='NR' is chosen *and* to know how many MATCHCOLS exist for each leg. The order in the PLAN_TABLE will be the sequence that is coded in the SQL. This allows the customer to match the PLAN_TABLE to the SQL. The actual order of execution will depend on the literal values used at runtime.

OUTER JOIN merge and subquery improvements

In general, materialization is more expensive for the execution of an SQL statement compared with merging a view or table expression. Therefore, in each release, DB2 continues to extend cases where MERGE occurs instead of materialization, and DB2 10 for z/OS is no exception.

When there are CASE, VALUE, COALESCE, NULLIF, or IFNULL expressions on the preserved side of an OUTER JOIN, DB2 will be enhanced to merge the view/table expression. The merge is blocked if it would result in a stage 2 predicate, such as a CASE expression in the ON clause.

Thus, the SQL in Figure 2.9 will merge the A table expression in DB2 10, while table expression B will continue to materialize. Prior to DB2 10, both table expressions will materialize.

```
SELECT A.C1, B.C1, A.C2, B.C2
FROM T1, (SELECT COALESCE(C1, 0) as C1 ,C2
            FROM T2 ) A  <--table expression A will be merged
         LEFT OUTER JOIN
              (SELECT COALESCE(C1, 0) as C1 ,C2
                 FROM T3 ) B   <--B will be materialized
           ON A.C2 = B.C2
WHERE T1.C2 = A.C2;
```

Figure 2.9: OUTER JOIN merge/materialization example

The second **OUTER JOIN** merge enhancement involves a view or table expression containing a subquery. Figure 2.10 provides an SQL example of a subquery on the NULL-supplied table of a **LEFT OUTER JOIN**. In DB2 10, this table expression (or view) can be merged to the **ON** clause.

```
SELECT *
FROM T1 LEFT OUTER JOIN
         (SELECT * FROM T2
            WHERE T2.C1 = (SELECT MAX(T3.C1) FROM T3)) TE <--subquery
ON T1.C1 = TE.C1;
```

↓

```
SELECT *
FROM T1 LEFT OUTER JOIN T2    <--table expression is merged
ON T2.C1 = (SELECT MAX(T3.C1) FROM T3)    <--subquery ON-predicate
AND T1.C1 = TT.C1;
```

Figure 2.10: OUTER JOIN with subquery merge example

These views and table expressions must contain a reference to only one table. DB2 performs the merge by converting the subquery predicate to a "before join" predicate—in the ON clause of a NULL-supplied table. When the table in the table expression is very large or there is significant filtering from the preserved side (left side of a **LEFT OUTER JOIN**), performance will be improved due to lack of materialization.

Note

Coding a subquery in an **ON** clause is *not* permitted. However, DB2 can merge the original table expression and execute as if this was coded.

If the table expression with subquery is on the preserved row table (left side of a LEFT OUTER JOIN), DB2 will merge the table expression with subquery to the WHERE clause to apply before the join. Coding a subquery in the WHERE clause for a preserved row table (left side of LEFT OUTER JOIN) is valid syntax, and users can code this themselves.

Correlated subquery to non-correlated rewrite

Although not strictly related to materialization, the following subquery rewrite enhancement is likely to be the most common query pattern of any of the previously discussed SQL examples within the merge/materialization topic.

The SQL shown in Figure 2.11 seeks to return the most recent transaction for a given ACCOUNTNO (hence the MAX subquery). It is common to see this type of operation coded as a correlated subquery.

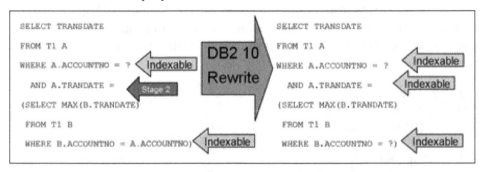

Figure 2.11: Correlated subquery to non-correlated rewrite example

Although the predicates on ACCOUNTNO in the outer query and the subquery are each indexable, the comparison of A.TRANDATE with the subquery result is stage 2, which means all transactions for a given account must be retrieved from the outer table.

DB2 10 can rewrite this construct to a non-correlated subquery if it is semantically equivalent. Therefore, the subquery will be executed before accessing the outer query block, and the subquery result would become indexable. DB2 could then choose two matching columns on the outer, and only the desired transaction would need to be accessed.

Stage 2 predicate pushdown

Stage 2 predicates are the most expensive for DB2 to apply. This message has been repeated for many years, and customers have been encouraged to rewrite stage 2 predicates to be stage 1 and/or indexable where possible.

Of course, not all SQL is under the control of developers who heed the recommendation, or the SQL may be application-generated. Also, not all stage 2 predicates are easily rewritten to a more efficient form. So, it is clear that DB2 cannot ignore the performance challenge.

DB2 10 enhances predicate application by enabling index manager and data manager (stage 1) to call Relational Data Services, or RDS (stage 2) to evaluate stage 2 predicates. Therefore, these predicates can potentially be applied as index screening before data page access.

Note
These pushed-down predicates cannot be applied as index matching. Index on expression (delivered in DB2 9 for z/OS) should be considered for index matching of stage 2 expressions.

This enhancement applies to arithmetic and date-time expressions, scalar built-in functions, and CAST operations. Limitations include:

* OR predicates must be able to be applied all at the same stage.
* Access paths involving list prefetch are not candidates for predicate pushdown.
* CASE expressions are not supported.
* IN-list predicates are not supported.

If the query qualifies, the predicates will be marked in the DSN_FILTER_TABLE under the column PUSHDOWN. The DSN_FILTER_TABLE is one of the extended explain tables; the manual *DB2 10 for z/OS Managing Performance* (SC19-2978) provides further details.

Figure 2.12 shows examples that demonstrate the eligibility for stage 2 predicate pushdown.

```
Suppose an index exists on (C1,C3):

• WHERE SUBSTR(C1,1,1) = ?                    ==> index screening

• WHERE SUBSTR(C1,1,1) = ? OR   C3 = ?        ==> index screening

• WHERE SUBSTR(C1,1,1) = ? OR   C4 = ?        ==> stage 1

• WHERE SUBSTR(C1,1,1) = ? AND  C4 = ?        ==> index screening and stage 1

• WHERE SUBSTR(C1,1,1) = ? OR C3 = (SELECT...)    ==> stage 2

• WHERE SUBSTR(C1,1,1) = ? AND C3 = (SELECT...)   ==> index screening
                                                      and stage 2
```

Figure 2.12: Stage 2 predicate pushdown examples

Based on the figure, where an index exists on C1,C3, prior to DB2 10 the SUBSTR predicate was always stage 2. In DB2 10, the following describes the eligibility of each predicate shown in the figure:

- WHERE SUBSTR(C1,1,1) = ?

  ○ Becomes an index screening candidate

- WHERE SUBSTR(C1,1,1) = ? OR C3 = ?

  ○ Despite the OR predicate, this is an index screening candidate because both sides of the OR can be applied at the same stage—as index screening.

- WHERE SUBSTR(C1,1,1) = ? OR C4 = ?

  ○ This example is *not* an index screening candidate because the predicate on C4 must be applied on the data row because it is not contained in the index. The compound predicate can, however, be pushed down to stage 1.

- WHERE SUBSTR(C1,1,1) = ? AND C4 = ?

  ○ The SUBSTR expression is an index screening candidate because it is not separated by OR and is therefore applied independently of the predicate on C4.

- WHERE SUBSTR(C1,1,1) = ? OR C3 = (SELECT . . .)

  ○ This is not an index screening candidate because predicates are separated by OR, and the subquery is not a candidate for pushdown. Thus, both predicates remain stage 2.

- WHERE SUBSTR(C1,1,1) = ? AND C3 = (SELECT . . .)

  ○ The subquery is stage 2, but because the predicates are separated by AND, the SUBSTR becomes an index screening candidate.

This predicate pushdown enhancement does require a REBIND to take effect.

Predicate simplification

Despite the eligibility to push down stage 2 predicates to an earlier stage, the fact remains that stage 2 predicates are the least efficient predicates for DB2 to apply. To clarify, it is still true that a stage 1 predicate is more efficient to apply than a stage 2 predicate that is pushed down to stage 1.

In recognition of some important query patterns for customers migrating from other platforms, DB2 V8 and V9 introduced several enhancements to predicate REWRITE that were enabled by ZPARM PREDPRUNE. Since few customers enabled the ZPARM, these enhancements do not become available for most customers until DB2 10, where the ZPARM is removed.

The first enhancement is to remove simple "always false" predicates. The targeted example is demonstrated in Figure 2.13.

```
WHERE ('A' = 'B' OR COL1 IN ('B', 'C'))
                    ↓
       WHERE COL1 IN ('B', 'C')
```

Figure 2.13: "Always false" predicate simplification

The always false 'A'='B' predicate renders the entire OR predicate stage 2. In DB2 10 (or V8/V9 with ZPARM PREDPRUNE enabled), the always false predicate will be removed, leaving the indexable predicate WHERE COL1 IN ('B', 'C').

Why would anyone code the original predicate? This query pattern came from a query generator, where this construct was used to enable or disable predicates within a common framework to simplify query generation.

For simplicity, assume I have two predicates and the user may want to search by only one or the other, or by both. If the user wants to search by LASTNAME, for example, the code generator would create the following predicates:

```
WHERE ('A' = 'B' OR LASTNAME = 'PURCELL')
  AND ('A' = 'A' OR CITY = 'ZZZZZ')
```

In this example, only the LASTNAME predicate is relevant. For each WHERE clause predicate to be true, one side of the OR must be true. Because 'A'='B' is false, LASTNAME='PURCELL' must be true for the row to qualify. And because 'A'='A' is true, it is irrelevant what the result is for the other side of the OR (CITY='ZZZZZ').

Thus, to enable the CITY predicate, the query generator would create the following predicate structure:

```
WHERE ('A' = 'A' OR LASTNAME = 'ZZZZZZ')
  AND ('A' = 'B' OR CITY = 'NEW YORK')
```

Now, the LASTNAME predicate has been "disabled," and the CITY predicate "enabled."

If you have read through these predicate pruning examples and have understood this construct, you will realize that this is another variation of coding a generic SQL to cover all potential search combinations. Other common solutions include coding all predicates as BETWEEN or LIKE predicates and setting the values to cover the full range if a value is not required—although only the aforementioned query pattern is the target of this enhancement.

Are you wondering what this means for documented tricks such as OR 0=1? OR 0=1 is not pruned, although other "always false" equal predicates such as OR 1=2 are pruned. And because this enhancement applies only to always false equal and IN predicates, any other false conditions, such as OR 1>2 or OR 0<>0, are not pruned.

Note

This enhancement applies only to literal values, not to parameter markers or host variables. Nor does it apply when **REOPT** is used with parameter markers or host variables.

Removing unnecessary tables

Continuing the theme of query simplification and removing redundancy from the query, an additional enhancement under the guise of **PREDPRUNE** in DB2 V8/V9 and enabled by default in DB2 10 is the removal of unnecessary tables in outer joins.

An **OUTER JOIN** is generally coded because the join relationship between two or more tables is optional. And while an **INNER JOIN** will only return rows that match across the join, an **OUTER JOIN** allows rows to be returned even if a match across the join is not found.

So, imagine you were to code a **LEFT OUTER JOIN** but not select any columns or apply filtering based on the result from that optional table. If the join does not introduce duplicates, then that table join was redundant.

Figure 2.14 shows an example of a redundant or unnecessary table join.

```
SELECT DISTINCT T1.C3
FROM T1 LEFT OUTER JOIN T2
ON T1.C2 = T2.C2
WHERE T1.C1 = ?
        ↓
SELECT DISTINCT T1.C3
FROM T1
WHERE T1.C1 = ?
```

Figure 2.14: Removing unnecessary tables from OUTER JOINs

Because this query selects only from T1, and no duplicates can be introduced by the join because of the **DISTINCT** in the query, the join to T2 is unnecessary, and DB2 will prune that table from the query with this new enhancement.

If a **DISTINCT** is not coded on the query, the table is considered redundant only if the join columns have a unique index guaranteeing that duplicates cannot be introduced by the join.

Note

If DB2 recognizes this pattern and removes tables from the query, these tables will not appear in the **PLAN_TABLE** output.

Sort Performance Enhancements

Now, let's move on from predicate processing to runtime optimizations related to sort. Sort is often an area of contention in query processing because sort is required for all workloads from online transaction processing (OLTP) through to reporting and business intelligence (BI) queries. And these queries are all competing for the same buffer pool resources and sort work data sets.

DB2 9 for z/OS introduced numerous enhancements to improve the efficiency of sort, and these improvements have been extended further in DB2 10 for z/OS.

For a query with ORDER BY plus FETCH FIRST n ROWS ONLY, if a sort for ORDER BY cannot be avoided with the use of an index, sorting a large result set can be inefficient when only a small number of rows are fetched.

In DB2 9, an in-memory replacement technique is used to achieve the desired order if the result is guaranteed to fit in a 32K page. In DB2 10, this support is extended to 128K.

Figure 2.15 demonstrates an example of the in-memory replacement sort that was introduced in DB2 9 for FETCH FIRST n ROWS ONLY queries that require order (ORDER BY is coded).

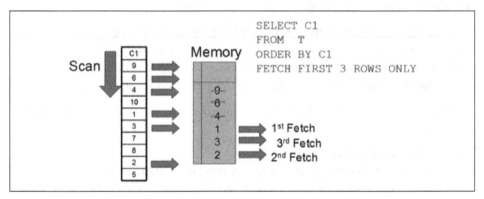

Figure 2.15: In-memory replacement sort

As the data is scanned, the ordered result is stored in-memory. As a new value is found that deserves to be in the first *n* rows, this value is swapped in and the highest stored value is swapped out. This process continues until all rows are processed by the chosen access path. Finally, the rows are returned in the required order.

To calculate whether this in-memory replacement technique will be used, multiply *n* (where *n* is the value specified by FETCH FIRST n ROWS ONLY) times the data row length and sort key (for ORDER BY or GROUP BY). (It should be noted that EXPLAIN does not show which sort technique was used.)

DB2 9 also avoids allocating a physical work file for final sort (for GROUP BY, ORDER BY, and DISTINCT) if the number of rows from sort is less than 256 and the result can fit in a 32K page. DB2 10 extends this support to intermediate sort in many situations.

Finally, GROUP BY queries with less than 32,000 groups will benefit from a hash assist to the input to sort. This allows rows to be hashed to the same location as other keys of the same value upon input to the sort process. Thus, it is more likely that the sort will be able to be completed in one MERGE pass, reducing work file usage for sort and improving performance.

All of the above-mentioned sort enhancements are considered runtime optimizations, and therefore explain is not aware whether these will take place.

New Choices for the Query Optimizer

As we've discussed, the DB2 optimizer must continually evolve, both with new choices in response to challenging query patterns and with cost model changes in response to the evolution of query workloads and associated performance challenges experienced by existing customers. Because our customers have grown accustomed to certain optimizer behavior from their existing workloads, one challenge is to ensure that the gradual evolution of improvements does not greatly disturb this balance.

Minimizing optimizer challenges for the optimizer cost model

Query performance regressions are, unfortunately, a possibility with any database management system. Fortunately for our DB2 for z/OS customers, their experiences are that regressions represent a very small percentage of their workload.

The reasons why cost-based optimization may not *always* generate the optimal plan include the following:

- Insufficient statistics
- Unsubstantiated query optimization assumptions due to lack of knowledge of actual values to be used at execution time
- Unpredictable runtime resource availability (e.g., RID pool usage and other concurrent activity)

In all, the plan picked by purely cost-based optimization may lack some robustness to prepare for various scenarios on some queries. To deal with some uncertainties, DB2 10 for z/OS begins to introduce the concept of risk into the cost estimation process. The optimizer can choose the plan that has the lowest risk associated with it, within the range of access paths that are considered close to the lowest cost.

The simplest example is for the optimizer to answer the question, "How many rows qualify WHERE BIRTHDATE < ?" Because the predicate is a parameter marker or host variable, the optimizer cannot accurately estimate the selectivity of the predicate until the literal value is known, since it is entirely possible that anywhere from 0 percent to 100 percent of the rows could qualify, depending on the value used at execution time.

Because a majority of queries use parameter markers or host variables, this type of predicate remains a challenge for the optimizer to estimate accurately. DB2 10 considers the risk of the estimate associated with such a predicate in its cost estimation. This enhancement is not something that can be controlled by customers, and it is an enhancement to the internal optimizer cost model to help choose an access path that has both the lowest cost and lowest risk.

Minimizing risk of RID failure

Another area of risk for execution performance regression is when the optimizer chooses a list prefetch plan and an inaccurate estimation results in a record identifier (RID) pool overflow or other RID limit reached due to concurrent query activity. When this happens, RID access falls back to a table space scan and all index filtering is lost.

Historically, the DB2 optimizer performs RID threshold checking as part of query optimization to avoid this runtime performance degradation. However, the optimizer may mistakenly estimate the number of qualified rows, or many concurrent queries may compete for the RID resources. Either of these situations could cause a limit to be reached.

DB2 10 for z/OS is enhanced to fail over to writing the RIDs to a work file and continue RID processing rather than falling back to table space scan in many situations.

A ZPARM, MAXTEMPS_RID, controls the maximum amount of work file usage for RID processing. However, we recommend you use this parameter as a safety net rather than as a general-use setting. The recommendation to use the default is to avoid a scenario of reaching a RID threshold and failing over to a work file and continuing processing, only to reach the ZPARM limit and finally fall back to table space scan.

Hybrid join already supports incremental RID processing once a RID limit is reached, and DB2 9 dynamic index ANDing already supports writing RIDs to a work file instead of falling back to table space scan. Therefore, the major targets for this enhancement are list prefetch and multi-index access. There still exist cases where fallback to table space scan will occur, such as queries involving column functions (MAX, MIN, and so on).

To reduce the incidences of RID pool overflow, DB2 10 also increases the RID pool default (ZPARM MAXRBLK) from 8 MB to 400 MB.

OPTIMIZE FOR 1 ROW fix

It has been documented for many releases that OPTIMIZE FOR 1 ROW (OF1R) will try to choose an access path that avoids a sort in an effort to return the first row quickly. DB2 Development received requirements from DB2 9 and DB2 10 beta customers to strengthen this OF1R sort avoidance behavior based on customers seeing some queries choose an access path that sorted when OF1R was coded. This is because the implementation of OF1R encouraged a sort avoidance plan but still allowed a cost-based decision for a sort path to be chosen if estimated to be efficient.

These requirements led to an enhancement to DB2 10 before GA for the optimizer to block sort plans if OF1R was coded (unless, of course, no sort avoidance plans existed).

A year after GA, a small number of customers saw access path regressions where OF1R queries switched from matching index access plus sort to a sort avoidance plan that was less efficient. For example, DB2 may have chosen a non-matching index scan to avoid the sort instead of the matching index plan that sorted. Non-matching index scan can be an inefficient choice if a large number of rows need to be scanned to find the first row that qualifies against the WHERE clause predicates.

Figure 2.16 demonstrates this challenge.

```
IDX1 (FIRSTNAME)
IDX2 (LASTNAME, FIRSTNAME)

SELECT *
FROM PHONEBOOK
WHERE FIRSTNAME = ?
ORDER BY LASTNAME, FIRSTNAME
OPTIMIZE FOR 1 ROW
```

Figure 2.16: OPTIMIZE FOR 1 ROW example

In this example, should the optimizer choose to match on IDX1 and sort? Or should it choose non-matching index scan (with index screening on FIRSTNAME) and avoid the sort using IDX2? The answer (unfortunately) is data dependent.

Let's use the first names of two recent U.S. presidents as an example to demonstrate.

WHERE FIRSTNAME='GEORGE' may return many rows with IDX1 and thus sort this larger number of rows to retrieve the first qualified row by LASTNAME, FIRSTNAME order. But a non-matching index will avoid the sort and find the first 'GEORGE' early in the scan, thus avoiding processing and sorting a large number of rows.

However, FIRSTNAME='BARACK' is likely to scan a large percentage of IDX2 before finding a match due to this being an uncommon first name. This means IDX1 is a safer choice for this example because it will match to find all occurrences of FIRSTNAME='BARACK' quickly, and because a small number of rows are likely to qualify, the sort will be efficient.

From this customer experience, we learned that we have two potential users of OF1R:

- Customers who used OF1R to guarantee sort avoidance (and/or avoidance of list prefetch and so on) for targeted queries
- Customers who may have used OF1R more pervasively (perhaps because it was adopted as a site standard for online transactions, or to solve a one-time query performance issue that has now gone, or by programmers inadvertently copying SQL that included the OF1R clause)

APAR PM56845 adds ZPARM OPT1ROWBLOCKSORT, which controls OF1R behavior. The parameter's default value is DISABLE, meaning that the optimizer tries to choose an access path that avoids a sort if it is estimated to be cost-effective in returning the first row quickly. However, the optimizer is free to consider plans that require a sort. Setting OPT1ROWBLOCKSORT to ENABLE disables plans that require a sort and chooses the lowest-cost plan that avoids a sort. The DISABLE setting is more consistent with the behavior of OF1R prior to DB2 10.

Extending VOLATILE TABLE usage

Another option widely used by customers to influence a particular optimizer behavior is the VOLATILE table attribute. VOLATILE table support was added in DB2 for z/OS Version 8 based on a requirement from SAP to support its cluster tables. The requirement was to always prefer index access over a table space scan, and to guarantee that the data rows would be accessed in the index sequence, which meant no list prefetch.

Many customers have true volatile tables—where the data volumes grow and shrink continually—making it difficult to collect a representative and reliable set of RUNSTATS data. However, these true volatile data tables do not always fit the SAP model for VOLATILE. The limitation on list prefetch would cause index access to be avoided if the only matching index plan required list prefetch.

DB2 10 for z/OS extends the VOLATILE table support to the general-use case, without impacting the SAP case. To do this, if a table has only one index and that index is unique, DB2 10 will continue to follow the original SAP cluster table rules. Because SAP cluster tables have only one index—and that index is defined as unique—this rule in DB2 10 lets the SAP-specific behavior be preserved.

If the table has more than one index (or the only index is non-unique), DB2 uses the NPGTHRSH ZPARM rules, which prioritize matching index access over table space scan or non-matching index scan. With NPGTHRSH, list prefetch is permitted.

Note

The goal of both VOLATILE (at the table level) and NPGTHRSH (at the subsystem level) is to choose the index with the most matching predicates. If multiple indexes have the same high matching columns, then these indexes compete on cost. There is still a benefit to attempting to collect representative statistics on VOLATILE tables because this information will be used in the optimizer cost-based decision.

Index INCLUDE columns

While not strictly related to the optimizer, the following enhancement can improve query performance if used correctly and also simplify the choices available to the optimizer. The enhancement is index INCLUDE column support, which has been a longstanding requirement from customers.

It is very common to see customers create indices to support index-only access. However, before DB2 10, for cases where you add columns to a unique index, customers are required to keep two indices: one to support the uniqueness of the business rule and the other to support index-only access.

In Figure 2.17, assume IDX1 guarantees the uniqueness of C1 and IDX2 is created to provide index-only access for some queries. In DB2 10, you can alter IDX1 to add C2 as an INCLUDE column and then drop IDX2. Or, you can create a new index as IDX3 UNIQUE (C1) INCLUDE (C2) and then drop the original indexes, IDX1 and IDX2. Regardless of the method used, the goal as demonstrated in the figure is to consolidate the two existing indexes into one.

```
IDX1 UNIQUE (C1)
IDX2 (C1,C2)

        ↓

Consolidate to
IDX1 UNIQUE (C1) INCLUDE (C2)
```

Figure 2.17: Index INCLUDE columns

Columns that are included cannot be matching columns for queries and cannot provide ordering for GROUP BY or ORDER BY. However, since the preceding columns are unique, matching on all columns preceding the included columns will guarantee one row or less is returned.

Therefore, while some queries may see a reduction in matching columns if there are predicates on all columns of the larger index, no measurable performance difference is expected.

Note

The true motivation for this enhancement is to reduce the number of indices on a table where additional indices have been added for index-only. Fewer indices can improve INSERT/UPDATE/DELETE and utility performance, reduce space, and potentially improve buffer pool hit ratios because fewer indices are competing for buffer pool resources.

The following comment should seem obvious, but adding more columns to an index increases the size of that index. And, therefore, adding INCLUDE columns may degrade the performance of queries that were previously using the original (smaller) index.

Improving Parallelism Efficiency and Removing Limitations

The introduction of System z9 Integrated Information Processor (zIIP) processors has increased the motivation for many customers to exploit parallelism. This is in addition to the traditional reason for parallelism, which is to reduce the elapsed time of long-running queries. DB2 10 continues the theme from prior releases of reducing parallelism limitations and also introduces enhancements to improve distribution of work across child tasks.

Removing parallelism limitations

In previous releases, when multi-row fetch is used, parallelism is disabled for the last parallel group in the top-level query block for many queries. For example, for the simple query SELECT * FROM TABLE, if multi-row fetch is used, parallelism is disabled. This restriction forces customers to choose between multi-row fetch and parallelism. Alternatively, if the customer does attempt both, DB2 may choose to introduce a final sort, if possible, so that parallelism and multi-row fetch can coexist.

DB2 10 removes this restriction of multi-row fetch and parallelism, but only if the query explicitly contains the FOR FETCH/READ ONLY clause. The restriction still exists for an ambiguous cursor (a query that is not explicitly a read-only query).

Another parallelism restriction removed in DB2 10 is when the parallel group contains a work file. In many situations, parallelism was disabled when a work file was contained within a parallel group. But in DB2 10, the work file can be shared across parallel child tasks. This enhancement applies only to CPU parallelism and does not extend to FULL OUTER JOINs.

Effectiveness of query parallelism

Once parallelism is chosen for a query, it is often a challenge for DB2 to ensure that the data is distributed evenly across each parallel child task. To effectively reduce the overall elapsed time of a query using parallelism, it is important for each child task to execute approximately the same amount of work; otherwise, the elapsed time is dictated by the single longest-running task.

The key ranges for each child task are decided at BIND/PREPARE time based on statistics such as LOW2KEY, HIGH2KEY, and/or histogram statistics. The optimizer assumes that the data is uniformly distributed throughout the range of LOW2KEY and HIGH2KEY, unless histogram statistics exist to provide more detail about the data distribution throughout the range. This makes DB2 too dependent on the availability and accuracy of the statistics. Because histograms are not generally collected by customers, the problem of uneven distribution of the parallel child tasks can be all too common.

This challenge of uneven distribution of the parallel child tasks is most evident when DB2 uses the index key ranges or IN-list elements to cut the parallel degrees. When parallelism degrees are cut based on page ranges or partition boundaries, the work is often more evenly distributed. Key range partitioning is used, in general, when the access path is driven by an available index—which is often desirable if this index also provides other predicate filtering.

Given the query in Figure 2.18, DB2 will consider the LOW2KEY and HIGH2KEY of the date column C1 and will distribute the keys across the number of degrees. At execution time, each parallel child task operates against its defined range of keys. But if the data is not evenly distributed across those key values, some parallel tasks may be processing fewer rows than other tasks—or zero rows.

```
SELECT *
FROM MEDIUM_TABLE M, LARGE_TABLE L
WHERE M.C2 = L.C2
AND M.C1 BETWEEN CURRENT DATE - 90 DAYS AND CURRENT DATE;
```

Figure 2.18: Sample query demonstrating the challenge in determining parallel ranges

Dynamic record range partitioning
DB2 10 for z/OS introduces *dynamic record range partitioning* to help address the problem of uneven distribution of the parallel child tasks. In dynamic record range partitioning, DB2 introduces a sort into the access path so that the exact number of rows and key values are known at execution time. The resultant rows from the sort will be divided evenly across the parallel child tasks for subsequent join operations.

This division of work doesn't have to be on the key boundary unless it is required to support GROUP BY or DISTINCT ordering. Record range partitioning is therefore dynamic because partitioning is no longer based on the key ranges decided at BIND/PREPARE time. Instead, the key ranges are based on the number of composite records and the number of work elements (parallel child tasks). All the problems associated with key partitioning, such as the limited number of distinct values, lack of statistics, data skew, and data correlation, are bypassed, and the composite side records are distributed evenly based on the actual number of rows sorted at query execution.

This sort is not free, however, and therefore the cost of the sort is taken into consideration by the optimizer in its cost-based access path decision.

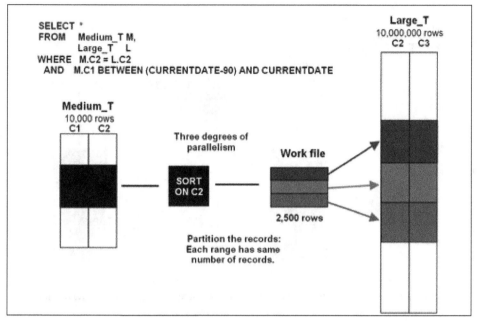

Figure 2.19: Dynamic record range partitioning example

Figure 2.19 provides an example of how the output of the sort is evenly distributed between the parallel child tasks, such that each child task processes the same number of rows for the next join step.

While this enhancement overcomes data skew or uneven distribution of work on the driving table in a join operation, it is still possible for subsequent joins to introduce a further unevenness to the number of rows being processed. And, as previously mentioned, dynamic record range partitioning is a new cost-based decision for the optimizer when parallelism is enabled for a query.

Straw model parallelism

The second solution in DB2 10 to deal with this uneven distribution challenge is *straw model parallelism*. The concept behind straw model is that DB2 will break up the access into more work elements than there are concurrent parallel degrees. And, therefore, with straw model, there is an opportunity to ensure that no single task is monopolizing the work.

For straw model, ZPARM PARAMDEG still drives the number of concurrent parallel degrees, but because more work elements are created, there is a queue of elements waiting. As each child task completes, it takes the next work element from the queue and begins processing.

In Figure 2.20, assume PARAMDEG is 3. The left side of the figure shows the work distributed without the benefit of straw model, and the right side demonstrates using straw model parallelism. For the straw model example, DB2 has chosen to create 10 work elements, with PARAMDEG=3 dictating the number that actually execute concurrently.

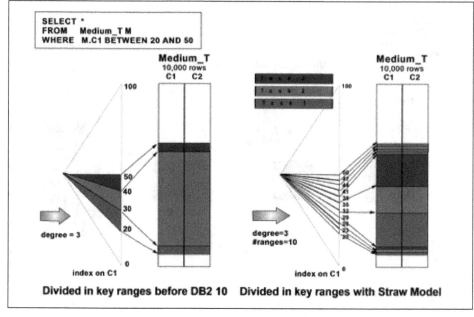

Figure 2.20: Straw model parallelism example

Note

The number of work elements is influenced by factors such as the number of partitions if parallelism cuts on page ranges or the number of keys if parallelism cuts on key ranges.

Thus, for the straw model example in the figure, tasks 1 to 3 will process the first three work elements. If child task 2 completes first, it will take the fourth work element (first in the queue) to begin processing. Next, if task 3 completes, it will take the fifth work element (next in the queue), and so on, until all work elements are complete.

This straw model process allows parallelism to cut the work into a finer degree of granularity. If the work is not distributed evenly, the shorter-running tasks will complete quicker and begin on the next element in the queue.

Cutting to a finer degree of granularity increases the likelihood that more tasks will share the work and avoids the situations where one task processes all the rows and other child tasks process zero rows.

Both straw model and dynamic record range partitioning are new cost-based choices available to the optimizer in DB2 10 for z/OS.

Improving the Inputs to the Query Optimizer

While a discussion on RUNSTATS is not technically an optimizer topic, the RUNSTATS utility is the method to capture the catalog statistics that the optimizer uses for access path selection. And, therefore, any enhancements to RUNSTATS may ease the burden associated with the statistics collection process and also improve the stability of access path choices.

When discussing RUNSTATS and the optimizer, it is common to hear the question, "When is the optimizer going to take advantage of real-time statistics (RTS)?" The simple answer is: in DB2 10.

But what needs an explanation is the other questions that also arise, such as, "When can I (or can I) stop running RUNSTATS and rely on RTS?" This question implies some misunderstanding of what information RUNSTATS and RTS can both provide to the DB2 optimizer.

In simple terms, RTS provides volume information—for example, how many INSERTs/UPDATEs/DELETEs have occurred since the last REORG or RUNSTATS—and for indexes, it reports how many pseudo-deleted index entries and near/far leaf pages exist.

While some of the optimizer decisions are based on object size (because it can cost more to access a one-million-row table than a ten-row table), the optimizer also needs to determine the selectivity of WHERE/ON clause predicates to estimate the cost associated with accessing each object. This means it needs column cardinalities (COLCARDF), frequencies/histograms, and more. And RTS does not provide this information.

Because the optimizer still relies on RUNSTATS, DB2 10 for z/OS also includes improvements to the usability and performance of the RUNSTATS utility.

Optimizer validation with real-time statistics

If real-time statistics doesn't provide all the information necessary for the optimizer, how does the optimizer use RTS in DB2 10 for z/OS? The simple answer is that RTS is being used as a "sanity check" for certain exception conditions.

The situations where the optimizer will validate the catalog statistics against RTS include:

- The catalog shows that the table, or the qualified partitions, are empty, or
- The table is marked as VOLATILE with default statistics, or
- The table qualifies for NPGTHRSH (NPAGESF < NPGTHRSH ZPARM).

In these scenarios, DB2 will read the RTS tables during static BIND/REBIND or dynamic PREPARE to validate the number of rows in the table. This value is then used in the optimizer's access path selection.

Note

Since RTS was integrated into the DB2 catalog in DB2 9 New Function Mode (NFM), customers migrating to DB2 10 from DB2 9 are able to exploit optimizer validation with RTS in DB2 10 Conversion Mode 9 (CM9). Customers migrating from DB2 V8 must wait until DB2 10 NFM before the optimizer can exploit RTS.

In addition to reading RTS, DB2 10 adds a further validation for WHERE clause predicates using a probe of index non-leaf pages for exception conditions. If a WHERE clause predicate is estimated by the optimizer to qualify zero rows and there exists an index that would support matching index access, DB2 will also probe the index non-leaf pages during BIND/PREPARE to validate the predicate estimate.

This index probing applies only if the optimizer has the literal value at BIND/PREPARE to use for the index probe. This means either the query must contain literals rather than host variables or parameter markers, or it must use the REOPT BIND parameter. RTS validation, however, does not require the literal values or REOPT to validate the number of rows in the table or partition.

This predicate and table size validation is externalized in a new EXPLAIN table called the DSN_COLDIST_TABLE.

RUNSTATS problem summary and automation

Understanding what RUNSTATS options to collect, and when to collect them, is a complex task. Answering the question, "When to collect statistics?" has been made easier with the stored procedure DSNACCOX.

But the second question—"What to collect?"—remains a challenging task without the benefit of some tooling. Fortunately, IBM has the Data Studio or Optim™ Query Workload Tuner Statistics Advisor as a standalone tool that can analyze a query or workload and determine which statistics would benefit.

In addition to the above solutions, which are already available, DB2 10 has taken steps to improve the automation of statistics collection.

The DB2 10 solution for automating statistics maintenance is through a set of stored procedures that can monitor the need for statistics collection and schedule the execution of RUNSTATS. The *DB2 10 for z/OS Managing Performance* guide contains a section titled "Automating statistics maintenance" that provides more detailed information, including the steps required to set up the monitoring.

This process will issue RUNSTATS alerts for out-of-date, missing, and conflicting database statistics. However, it should be noted that the process is *not* determining tailored RUNSTATS for your query workloads, which is the goal of a statistics advisor tool.

Once the required statistics are identified, executing RUNSTATS through this automated process can collect those statistics through the exploitation of statistics profiles, which we discuss in the next section.

Note

The goal of these stored procedures is to simplify integration with tooling provided by various vendors. However, this does *not* preclude a customer from integrating this process into their existing statistics collection process.

In addition to RUNSTATS automation, additional DB2 10 enhancements attempt to help with RUNSTATS complexity and cost.

RUNSTATS simplification

The first enhancement for RUNSTATS simplification is related to the KEYCARD option becoming the default for index RUNSTATS—regardless of whether it is explicitly specified. This change is in response to the ongoing recommendation by IBM for customers to collect KEYCARD to provide more accurate information to the optimizer about the intermediate multi-column cardinalities for indexes with three or more columns.

The general recommendation for statistics has been to collect RUNSTATS TABLE(ALL) INDEX(ALL) KEYCARD; now, with KEYCARD defaulted, the recommendation can be simplified to RUNSTATS TABLE(ALL) INDEX(ALL). A generalized recommendation for additional FREQVAL, HISTOGRAM, or COLGROUP statistics is more complicated, however, as the requirement for these additional statistics is based on predicates from an individual query or workload. This is why tooling is often necessary to assist in the identification of this requirement.

Once additional statistics requirements are identified, DB2 10 lets you create an individual statistics profile for each table such that the execution of RUNSTATS can simply use the option USE PROFILE to collect these targeted statistics for a table.

Figure 2.21 shows some examples of the statistics profile options in DB2 10.

Integrate specialized statistics into generic RUNSTATS job
- RUNSTATS ... TABLE tbl COLUMN(C1)... **SET PROFILE**
  Or use **SET PROFILE FROM EXISTING STATS**
- RUNSTATS ... TABLE tbl COLUMN(C5)... **UPDATE PROFILE**
- RUNSTATS ... TABLE tbl **USE PROFILE**

Figure 2.21: RUNSTATS options to SET/UPDATE/USE a stats profile

The statistics profile options include the ability to:

- SET PROFILE
- UPDATE PROFILE
- USE PROFILE
- DELETE PROFILE

When included in a RUNSTATS execution, SET, UPDATE, and DELETE do *not* physically execute the RUNSTATS job to collect statistics; they simply create, update, or delete the stored profile.

One nice feature of this statistics profile is the ability to SET PROFILE FROM EXISTING STATS. In this case, DB2 will create the statistics profile based on the statistics that exist in the catalog for this table. This feature can be beneficial if you have collected FREQVAL, HISTOGRAM, and/or COLGROUP at different times but do not have a record of all the options that have been used over time.

UPDATE PROFILE can merge the existing profile information with the new options when you want to add new options to a profile. If you want to truly replace the profile, it is preferable to perform a DELETE PROFILE followed by a new SET PROFILE.

The only concern with this approach is that deleting a profile does *not* delete existing statistics. Leaving statistics in the catalog that are no longer being re-collected will cause those statistics to become stale. Therefore, an additional step is to manually delete those statistics from the catalog that are no longer part of a profile.

The statistics profiles are not without their own usability challenges. When USE PROFILE is specified, all tables specified in the RUNSTATS job must have a profile. Therefore, if you have 10,000 objects to collect statistics on and only 50 have special-ized RUNSTATS requirements, you cannot integrate the 9,950 default RUNSTATS tables with the statistics profile tables. The current implementation of statistics profiles does, however, simplify the RUNSTATS syntax when issuing a single-table RUNSTATS.

RUNSTATS performance

The other important enhancement to RUNSTATS focuses on improving performance. The existing SAMPLE option of RUNSTATS can reduce CPU cost because it only performs the CPU-intensive cardinality calculation on the percentage specified by the SAMPLE keyword. However, regardless of the SAMPLE percentage specified, all 100 percent of the rows are still read by the RUNSTATS job.

DB2 10 adds the option to sample at the page/row level—which means a reduc-tion in the rows RUNSTATS will read. This enhancement can produce a more significant improvement in the CPU and elapsed time performance of RUNSTATS.

When given the option to choose a percentage, the most obvious question is, "What percentage to use?" DB2 provides the TABLESAMPLE SYSTEM AUTO option, which lets

DB2 choose the right percentage based on the table size. When you specify the AUTO option, tables with less than 500,000 rows will use a 100 percent sample, and after 500,000 rows, the percentage will scale down from 100 percent to a low value of 10 percent. RUNSTATS will adjust the percentage with the AUTO option, or you can override with a specific numeric value.

Being more aggressive with a lower-percentage SAMPLE value can reduce the RUNSTATS cost further. However, there is some risk of being too aggressive because RUNSTATS is unable to estimate the values for the rows that are skipped. For this reason, DB2 implements a lower value of 10 percent.

TABLESAMPLE applies only to single-table table spaces, and it is not applicable for LOB table spaces. Indexes do not exploit this page- and row-level sampling.

Summary

DB2 10 for z/OS is a significant release for query performance and optimization. The improvements in these areas are an acknowledgement of the increased focus our customers are placing on reducing total cost of ownership while maintaining the stability and reliability of their mainframe environments.

While prior releases of DB2 have brought new optimizer access path choices, this additional focus on predicate and runtime optimizations, and on plan management, should provide the goal of improved performance with lower risk than before—a focus that is expected to continue in future releases of DB2.

Planning for IBM DB2 10
for z/OS Upgrade

by John Campbell
IBM Silicon Valley Lab

This paper focuses on the *planning stage* of migrating to IBM DB2 10 for z/OS. The key points of emphasis are:

✓ Make sure everyone is educated as to what is needed to ensure project success.
✓ Production of a detailed project plan, communicated to all involved, is crucial for success.
✓ Some preparation can occur very early, in terms of understanding, obtaining, and installing the prerequisites.

The release of DB2 10 for z/OS was announced on February 9, 2010, and the product began shipping on March 12, 2010. It was the largest beta test program in the history of DB2 for z/OS.

The information in this paper is drawn from the lessons learned in cooperation with some of IBM's largest customers, both during the beta program and during production deployment since DB2 10 for z/OS became generally available.

Many of IBM's largest customers were looking mainly for 31-bit virtual storage constraint relief in the DBM1 address space, as well as to exploit all the opportunities available for price/performance improvement. Other areas of interest included:

• Regression testing *(Be sure to approach regression testing in the order in which you plan to move to production.)*
• "Out-of-the-box" performance
• Additional performance improvements
• Scalability enhancements
• New functions such as Temporal Data and many others

Stages of migration

The primary stages of migration to a new version are:

1. Planning

   ○ Early stages:
      » Making the decision to migrate
      » Determining what can be gained
      » Planning for prerequisites
      » Avoiding incompatibilities
      » Planning performance and storage
      » Assessing available resources

2. Migration
3. Implementation of the new improvements

Needed application changes can be made over a longer period to make the migration process easier and less costly. Plans for monitoring virtual and real storage resource consumption, as well as performance, are necessary. An early health check, communication of the required changes, and staging of the work will make the project go much more smoothly.

Highlights of the Beta Program Testing

DB2 10 for z/OS delivers great value by *reducing CPU resource consumption in most customer cases*. IBM internal testing and early beta customer results revealed that, depending on the specific workload, many customers could achieve *"out-of-the-box" DB2 CPU resource consumption savings of up to 10 percent* for traditional online transaction processing (OLTP) workloads and *up to 20 percent for specific new workloads (e.g., native SQL procedures)*, compared with running the same workloads on DB2 9 for z/OS or DB2 for z/OS Version 8.

The objective of providing and proving generous, 31-bit virtual storage constraint relief in the DBM1 address space was achieved by the end of the program. This achievement is significant in terms of providing for the enhanced vertical scalability of an individual DB2 subsystem or DB2 member of a data sharing group. We are confident that customers can scale up, in practical terms, the number of active threads by 5 to 10 times to meet their demands.

Further opportunities for price/performance improvement are made possible through the use of persistent threads running with packages bound with the BIND option RELEASE(DEALLOCATE). Examples of using persistent threads include protected ENTRY threads with Customer Information Control System (CICS®), Wait For Input (WFI) regions with Information Management System/Transaction Manager (IMS™/TM), and high-performance database access threads (DBATs) for incoming Distributed Data Facility (DDF) workloads.

Another goal was to improve INSERT performance, particularly in the area of universal table spaces (UTSs). We wanted to ensure that insert performance for UTS was equal to, or better than, the classic table space types, such as segmented and partitioned. This goal was achieved in most cases.

Hash access was good, provided we hit the smaller-than-expected "sweet spot." Results for complex queries were also good.

Provided users made a good choice for the size of the inline portion, the performance of inline large objects (LOBs) was also impressive. Support for inline LOB column values has the potential to save on performance by avoiding indexed access to the auxiliary table space. However, it is important to note that the value you choose for the inline LOB portion must ensure that most of the LOB column values are 100 percent inline in the base table space.

In the area of latch contention reduction, we focused on the hot latches in DB2 10 for z/OS in such a way that, once we solved the 31-bit virtual storage constraint issue in the DBM1 address space, enabling you to scale up 5 to 10 times in terms of threads, we wanted to be sure there were no secondary issues related to latch contention that would inhibit the vertical scalability of a single DB2 subsystem or DB2 member of a data sharing group.

As the beta program progressed, the reliability of, and customer confidence in, DB2 10 for z/OS greatly improved.

Generally speaking, OLTP performance improvements achieved were as predicted. We were aiming for an aggressive target of 5 percent to 10 percent reduction in CPU resource consumption for most traditional OLTP workloads. During testing, several customers ran benchmarks showing that such reductions could be achieved. However, in cases where the transactions consisted of a few very simple SQL statements, the 5 percent to 10 percent target was not achieved. This is where the increase in package allocation cost outweighed the improvement in SQL runtime optimization. However, we did identify some steps that can be taken to improve this. We have delivered an Authorized Program Analysis Report (APAR) to reduce package allocation cost. It is also possible to mitigate this situation by making more use of persistent threads running such packages bound with the BIND option RELEASE(DEALLOCATE).

Another issue was single-thread BIND/REBIND performance. Even in Conversion Mode (CM), the performance, in terms of CPU resource consumption and elapsed time, was degraded. One reason for this result was that in DB2 10 for z/OS, the default for access plan stability is EXTENDED. Also, DB2 10 for z/OS uses indexed access, even in CM, to access the respective DB2 catalog and directory tables.

Another area where we had mixed results was SQL Data Definition Language (DDL) concurrency. We had hoped that by restructuring the DB2 catalog and directory to introduce row-level locking, remove hash link access, and more, we could improve concurrency when running parallel SQL DDL and parallel **BIND/REBIND** operations. The concurrency improvement was eventually achieved for parallel **BIND/REBIND** activity. Although it also helped in some cases with SQL DDL, most customers will still have to run SQL DDL activity single-threaded.

The final issue was access path lockdown. Two new options in DB2 10 for z/OS, **APREUSE** and **APCOMPARE**, enable you to generate a new SQL runtime while in most cases keeping the old access paths. Unfortunately, there were some issues with the underlying **OPTHINTS** infrastructure inherited by DB2 10 for z/OS, which is used by **APREUSE** and **APCOMPARE**. The introduction of **APREUSE** and **APCOMPARE** was delayed until these issues were addressed. These features are now available in the service stream via APARs and are working very well in real customer environments; their use is strongly recommended.

In general terms, the results of the beta program were mainly positive customer experiences, and we received good feedback about the program. A majority of customers in the beta program plan started to migrate to DB2 10 for z/OS in 2011. We observed incremental improvement in the program over what we experienced previously with the DB2 9 for z/OS and DB2 for z/OS Version 8 programs.

There was really no "single voice" or message across the customer set. We saw significant variation in terms of customer commitment and achievement. A small subset of customers did a very good job on regression and new function testing and provided good feedback. Others, due to limited resources, were only able to provide limited qualification about what they were going to do and what they were able to achieve.

It is worth keeping in mind, for those who have never been involved in a Quality Partnership Program (QPP)/beta program, that it can be a challenge for customers to sustain the effort over a six-month period, due to competing business and technical priorities as well as constraints on people, hardware resources, and time.

By the end of the program, no customers were in true, business production. But we also need to appreciate that a QPP/beta program is *not* the same as an Early Support Program. We continue to develop and test the DB2 for z/OS product as the program progresses.

One of the benefits of DB2 10 for z/OS is that it provides many opportunities for price/performance (cost reduction) improvements. It is a major theme of this release. In discussions with customers, these opportunities for price/performance improvement are most welcome.

Also keep in mind that customers can be intimidated by some of the marketing "noise" about improved price/performance, often because of the raised expectation level of their respective CIOs. But in some cases, it is because when they run their own workloads, they do not see the anticipated improvements in reduced CPU resource consumption and improved elapsed time performance that they expected. Many customers saw big improvements for certain workloads, while for other workloads they saw little, if any, improvement.

Also note that if you have small test workloads that are untypical of the total mixed workload running in production, this can skew expectations on savings—either positively or negatively. Once DB2 10 for z/OS is in production, the results with the full, mixed workload may differ. We found that some measurements and quotes were overly positive and should be ignored.

A remaining question is: "How do you extrapolate from a small workload and project what the savings would be for the total, mixed workload in production?" Estimating with accuracy and high confidence is not practical, or possible, without proper benchmarking using a workload that truly represents production.

Overall, most of the customer testing identified opportunities for price/performance (cost savings) improvements, which is the major theme of this release. Some customers reported big improvements in CPU resource consumption and elapsed time reduction for certain workloads, while others did not. Keep in mind that smaller workloads may skew expectations on savings.

Summary of results

The DB2 10 for z/OS beta program confirmed improvements in the following areas:

- ✓ 31-bit virtual storage constraint relief in the DBM1 address space
- ✓ Insert performance
- ✓ Hash access good when hitting the smaller-than-expected sweet spot
- ✓ Complex queries
- ✓ Inline LOBs for short large objects ("SLOBs")
- ✓ Latch contention reduction
- ✓ Quality of problems and issues found
- ✓ Reliability and confidence as program progressed

Performance and Scalability

One of the key lessons learned in the beta program was the need to plan on additional real storage resource consumption. A 10 percent to 30 percent increase of real storage resource consumption is a very rough estimate. For small systems with tiny buffer pools, the increase will be toward the high end of the range; for big systems with large buffer pools, it will be toward the low end of the range. It is important for customers to properly provision and monitor real storage resource consumption.

This high-level guideline can be refined further to determine the additional requirement. Under DB2 9 for z/OS or DB2 for z/OS Version 8, collect IFCID 225 record data. Make sure the DB2 subsystem is properly warmed up so that virtual storage has been allocated to support normal DB2 operations. Extract the real and auxiliary storage usage

(QW0225RL and QW0225AX, respectively) from IFCID 225 records, subtract out the VPSIZE for all the local buffer pools, and add 30 percent to the remainder. Next, add in the increased virtual storage needed for increases in the default size for the sort and row ID (RID) pools, and then add in the increased requirement for MAXSPACE (from 9 GB to typically 16 GB under DB2 10 for z/OS). Compare this new value against the original value from DB2 9 for z/OS or DB2 for z/OS Version 8. Note carefully that if there is a non-zero value for auxiliary storage (QW0255AX), there may be some double counting on memory usage, as slots in auxiliary storage are still owned by a DB2 subsystem even though the set of pages is paged back in later. The slots in auxiliary storage continue to be owned by a DB2 subsystem until they are reused by another subsystem/user or the subject DB2 subsystem is shut down.

Many traditional OLTP workloads saw a 5 percent to 10 percent reduction in CPU resource consumption in CM mode after package REBIND under DB2 10 for z/OS (some more, some less). On the initial migration to DB2 10 for z/OS, most customers will not perform a mass REBIND of all plans and packages. So, before REBINDing plans and packages, you may see little or no reduction in CPU resource consumption.

To maximize the price/performance benefits after migrating to CM:

1. REBIND your migrated packages and plans to generate the new optimized 64-bit SQL runtime. This way, you avoid the overhead of converting the run-time structures for migrated packages from earlier releases to look like the DB2 10 for z/OS runtime structures. Re-enable fast column (SPROC or SELECT Processing) processing, which would otherwise be disabled.

2. Take advantage of 1 MB size real storage page frames to reduce translation lookaside buffer (TLB) misses. The 1 MB size real storage page frames are available on the z10™ and z196 processors. The prerequisite for using them is to specify the long-term page fix option for your local buffer pools. Long-term page fix buffer pools, which were introduced in DB2 for z/OS Version 8, provide an opportunity to reduce CPU resource consumption by avoiding the repetitive cost of page fix and page free operations for each page involved in an I/O operation.

The lesson is, be sure to use PGFIX=YES on your local buffer pools, provided there is sufficient real storage provisioned to fully back the requirement of the total normal DB2 working set below and above the 2 GB bar, plus have some spare available real storage capacity for MAXSPACE so that dumps can be taken very quickly to avoid disrupting the logical partition (LPAR), which could lead to "sympathy sickness" around the rest of the data sharing group.

In a few cases, customers saw less than 5 percent saving in CPU resource consumption for traditional OLTP with very light transactions—"skinny" packages with a few simple SQL statements. This result is due partly to the increasing cost of package allocation, which overrides the benefit of the SQL runtime optimizations. APAR PM31614 may solve this issue by improving package allocation performance. Another way to address this is to use persistent threads running packages bound with the BIND option RELEASE(DEALLOCATE), to amortize away the repetitive cost of package allocation/deallocation per transaction.

Regarding customers' measurements, keep in mind that—unlike the DB2 Lab environment, where a dedicated environment is used—customer measurements are typically performed in a shared environment, and the measurement results are not always consistent and repeatable. There can be wide variation on measurement "noise" in customer measurements, especially regarding elapsed time performance.

In most cases, customers were *not* running in a dedicated environment or at the scale/size of true business production. Many customers ran a subset (maybe a high-volume subset) of the total production workload. Sometimes, they used a synthetic test workload to study specific enhancements.

In cases where customers had very large savings that they were not able to reproduce, the numbers on CPU and elapsed time reductions were not trusted.

Recommendation

Customers should not spend anticipated price/performance (cost reduction) savings until they actually see the improvements in their own true business production environment.

Early results

Table 1.1 summarizes some of the beta program results reported by customers. Some of the additional savings were due to features such as using 1 MB size real storage page frames for selective buffer pools, enabling high-performance DBATs, and using the package BIND option RELEASE(DEALLOCATE). Another reason was the improvement in COMMIT processing for applications that commit frequently. We now perform parallel write I/O operations to the active log dataset pair even when rewriting a log control interval (CI) that was partially filled and written out previously.

Workload	Customer results
CICS online transactions	Approximately 7% CPU reduction in DB2 10 CM after REBIND; additional reduction when 1 MB size real storage page frames were used for selective buffer pools
CICS online transactions	Approximately 10% CPU reduction from DB2 9
CICS online transactions	Approximately 5% CPU reduction from DB2 for z/OS V8
CICS online transactions	10+% CPU increase
Distributed concurrent insert	50% DB2 elapsed time reduction; 15% chargeable CPU reduction after enabling high-performance DBAT
Data sharing heavy concurrent insert	38% CPU reduction
Queries	Average CPU reduction 28% from V8 to DB2 10 NFM
Batch	Overall 20–25% CPU reduction after rebind packages

Table 1.1: Workload results reported by DB2 10 for z/OS beta program customers

Now, let us discuss the use of the 1 MB size real storage page frames on the z10 and z196 processors. The potential exists for reduced CPU resource consumption through fewer TLB misses; however, the local buffer pools must be defined as long-term page fixed (PGFIX=YES). This feature was introduced in DB2 for z/OS Version 8 to mitigate CPU regression and reduce CPU resource consumption for I/O-intensive buffer pools.

Many customers are still reluctant to use the PGFIX=YES option because they are running too close to the edge on the usage of the amount of real storage provisioned on the LPAR and are in danger of paging to auxiliary (DASD) storage. They understand the value of PGFIX=YES, but the benefit may only apply for an hour or two each day. Another factor is that this decision is a long-term one; in most cases, implementing this buffer pool attribute requires a recycle of the DB2 subsystem to actually implement the change. A change to the subject attribute goes pending and is materialized when the buffer pool next goes through reallocation. It is also worth noting that there is a significant cost reduction for real storage on the z196 processor relative to the z10 processor. The cost saving is approximately 75 percent.

Here are a few more things to remember about the use of 1 MB size real storage page frames on the z10 and z196 processors: The actual amount of memory that is allocated as 1 MB size real storage page frames is specified by the LFAREA parameter in the IEASYSnn parmlib member and is changeable only by IPL. You are partitioning out the total real storage provisioned between 4K size frames and 1 MB size frames. 1 MB size real storage page frames are non-pageable. If these page frames are overcommitted, DB2 10 for z/OS will start using 4K size real storage page frames.

Do not be perturbed by z/OS issuing messages IRA120E (80 percent full) and IRA121E (95 percent full). These messages would appear to indicate a shortage in the large frame area (LFAREA). The ending "E" in the message identifiers actually means "eventual action" and not something that is actually wrong now. These messages are "informational" and do not indicate an "error" condition. The first message, "IRA120E – Large frame shortage," is generated when the definition of the PGFIX=YES buffer pools overruns the 80 percent cushion for the large frame area. To avoid these messages, an installation would have to define the LFAREA to be 20 percent larger than the sum of the local buffer pools marked as long-term page fixed. This would waste real storage unnecessarily. Assuming the sum of all the local buffer pools marked as long-term page fixed was 15 GB, then to have a 20 percent cushion for 15 GB means the LFAREA must be defined at approximately 19 GB. But the extra 4 GB real storage is then wasted because no subsystem other than DB2 can use the large frame area. These messages will be upgraded to "informational" messages via APAR OA39941 in z/OS V2R1. In the meantime, the IRA120E (80 percent full) and IRA121E (95 percent full) messages should be tolerated.

Recommendation

Assuming you have provisioned sufficient real storage in production LPAR to fully back the total requirement of the DB2 working set size, plus you have some spare available real storage capacity for the MAXSPACE requirement so that dumps can be taken very quickly to avoid disrupting the LPAR (which could lead to sympathy sickness around the rest of the data sharing group):

1. Define all the local buffer pools as long-term page fixed (PGFIX=YES).
2. Sum up the total buffer pool storage requirement across all the local buffer pools defined as PGFIX=YES.
3. Reflect that value in the LFAREA specification. (You may want to add an additional 5 percent to 10 percent in size to allow for some growth and tuning.)

Note

Make sure you have applied critical preventative z/OS maintenance before using 1 MB size real storage page frames. One of the lessons learned in the beta program is that the 1 MB size real storage page frames are relatively new, and DB2 10 for z/OS is the first major subsystem to exploit them. We observed a reduction of up to 6 percent in CPU resource consumption by using the 1 MB size real storage page frames. This improvement is over and above the benefit of long-term page fix for local buffer pools first introduced in DB2 for z/OS Version 8. There is a customer requirement for a new parameter to be able to use PGFIX=YES independently from the use of 1 MB size real storage page frames. This requirement will be addressed in a future release of DB2 for z/OS.

The 31-bit virtual storage constraint relief (VSCR) in the DBM1 address space with a near-complete 64-bit SQL runtime is available immediately for use as soon as you go to CM. To accrue maximum benefit, you must REBIND static SQL plans and packages. We are confident that we have addressed the previous vertical-scalability issue on the limited number of active threads that a single DB2 subsystem could support, and we have achieved very good results. This support offers a "real-world" proposition of scaling up the number of active threads from, say, 500 active threads to 2,500–3,000 active threads or more per DB2 subsystem. The limiting factors now on the vertical scalability of a DB2 subsystem (number of threads times average thread storage footprint) are most likely to be the amount of real storage provisioned on the LPAR, followed by extended system queue area/extended common service area (31-bit ESQA/ECSA) storage constraints and the active log write performance (output log buffer latch contention).

Figure 1.1 shows three sets of customer measurements.

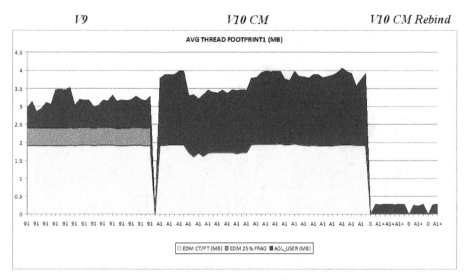

Figure 1.1: Initial DBM1 31-bit thread storage footprint customer measurements in DB2 9 for z/OS vs. DB2 10 for z/OS (corrected prior to General Availability [GA])

The first measurement (shown in the left column of the figure) is the 31-bit virtual storage thread footprint of DB2 9 for z/OS.

The middle column shows the virtual storage thread footprint of DB2 10 for z/OS in CM without the REBIND of static SQL plans and packages. The issue here is that the footprint actually increased, compared with DB2 9 for z/OS. Thankfully, this issue was identified during the beta program and was corrected ahead of GA of DB2 10 for z/OS.

The third column shows that once you do the REBIND of static SQL plans and packages, the 31-bit virtual thread storage footprint decreases dramatically. This result illustrates the value of the 31-bit virtual storage constraint relief in the DBM1 address space with DB2 10 for z/OS.

Figure 1.2 shows another group of customer measurements.

Here, the first column is the DB2 9 for z/OS 31-bit thread storage footprint. The second column is the 31-bit thread storage footprint for DB2 10 for z/OS CM without the REBIND of static SQL plans and packages. In columns three and four, you can see that after the fix is applied (even without the REBIND), the 31-bit thread storage footprint is greatly reduced.

With or without the REBIND of static SQL plans and packages, the 31-bit thread storage footprint in the DBM1 address space is reduced in DB2 10 for z/OS. However, to accrue maximum benefit in terms of 31-bit VSCR in the DBM1 address space, we strongly recommend implementing a program to progressively rebind all static SQL plans and

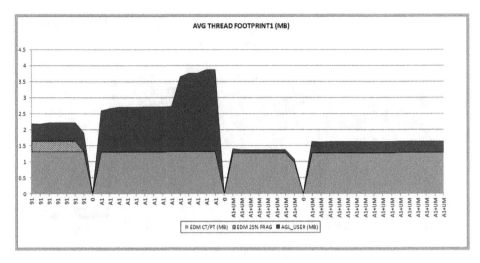

Figure 1.2. Initial DBM1 31-bit thread storage customer measurements
in DB2 9 for z/OS vs. DB2 10 for z/OS (GA after fix applied)

packages during the life of DB2 10 for z/OS. The program should start by rebinding the high-use packages, which represent a significant part of the total workload.

DBM1 virtual storage constraint relief with 64-bit SQL runtime

REBINDing static plans and packages maximizes the DBM1 31-bit VSCR and ensures we have a 64-bit SQL runtime. Not only does this step solve scalability issues, but it also can provide opportunities for further price/performance improvements—beyond the 5 percent to 10 percent.

For example, prior to DB2 10 for z/OS, many customers have been heavily constrained on available, 31-bit virtual storage in the DBM1 address space and, as a result, on the number of active threads that can be supported in a single DB2 subsystem or DB2 member. They have had to make compromises, trading additional CPU resource consumption to reduce the 31-bit virtual storage footprint and be able to support more active threads in a single DB2 subsystem or DB2 member.

This tradeoff involved reducing the number of persistent threads and restricting the use of packages bound with the BIND option RELEASE(DEALLOCATE) running on those threads. These tactics saved on 31-bit virtual storage resource consumption in the DBM1 address space at the cost of incurring additional CPU resource consumption.

With DB2 10 for z/OS, provided you have sufficient real storage provisioned on the LPAR over and above the 10 percent to 30 percent increased real storage resource consumption previously mentioned, you can use more persistent threads and make more use of packages bound with the BIND option RELEASE(DEALLOCATE) with the existing persistent threads or increased number of persistent threads defined. This capability has the potential to reduce CPU resource consumption and further improve price/performance (cost reduction) beyond the previously mentioned 5 percent to 10 percent. However, it will increase real storage resource consumption above the expected 10 to 30 percent increase on the initial migration to DB2 10 for z/OS as discussed previously. This may require additional real storage to be provisioned on the LPAR.

The next, and new, opportunity for price/performance improvement is with regard to Distributed Relational Database Architecture™ (DRDA) and DDF server workloads. In DB2 10 for z/OS, starting with CM there is the potential to reduce CPU resource consumption for DRDA transactions by using high-performance database access threads (high-performance DBATs). DB2 10 for z/OS provides the same opportunity for thread reuse with persistent threads running with packages bound with BIND option RELEASE(DEALLOCATE) that we have, for example, in CICS with protected ENTRY threads and/or by queuing on an unprotected ENTRY thread.

To take advantage of this improvement, the first prerequisite is that at least one of the packages associated with the transaction must be bound with RELEASE(DEALLOCATE). The second prerequisite is to issue the MODIFY DDF PKGREL(BNDOPT) command so that the BIND option RELEASE(COMMIT|DEALLOCATE) is respected.

After taking these steps, you will be able to achieve thread reuse for the same DDF connection. At the same time, DDF will start honoring the BIND option of RELEASE (DEALLOCATE). Before DB2 10 for z/OS, you could BIND the packages used by distributed workloads with the RELEASE(DEALLOCATE) option, but the availability of this option was a moot point because RELEASE(COMMIT) was always forced at execution time (in other words, the BIND option of RELEASE(DEALLOCATE) was not honored).

Now, in DB2 10 for z/OS, we have the same possibility as with CICS and IMS/TM workloads—to have persistent threads, in this case with high-performance DBATs, and to have the BIND option of RELEASE(DEALLOCATE) honored.

The recommendation is that before starting to use high-performance DBATs, you must plan on additional real storage resource consumption—beyond the previously discussed 10 percent to 30 percent increase, and you may have to provision additional real storage on the LPAR. *Do not* adopt a "one size fits all" strategy when using more persistent threads running with packages bound with the BIND option RELEASE(DEALLOCATE) with IMS/TM, CICS, or DDF workloads.

Most installations cannot support making all threads persistent, with all the associated packages running on the threads bound with the BIND option RELEASE(DEALLOCATE), because of the potential for dramatic increase in the total real storage resource consumption. Most installations simply cannot afford to use this option for all plans and packages.

Installations should target persistent threads for thread reuse at high-volume simple transactions and couple them with the use of BIND option RELEASE(DEALLOCATE) for high-use packages with many SQL statements that are frequently executed. For example, take your Open Database Connectivity (ODBC) and Java Database Connectivity (JDBC) packages as used by distributed client applications and BIND them twice—into two different package collections: BIND them with RELEASE(DEALLOCATE) in one collection (e.g., NULLID2), and BIND them with RELEASE(COMMIT) in the other collection (e.g., NULLID).

In this way, you can target the high-volume, web-based OLTP transaction workloads that would benefit most from the use of persistent threads running with packages bound with BIND option RELEASE(DEALLOCATE), and you can connect those applications to a data source that points to the collection (e.g., NULLID2) where the packages are bound with the BIND option RELEASE(DEALLOCATE). Packages bound with the BIND option RELEASE(DEALLOCATE) will be eligible to use high-performance DBATs and will be reused for the same connection. The remaining transaction and query workloads would connect to a data source that points to the collection (e.g., NULLID) where the packages are bound with RELEASE(COMMIT).

The story is similar with CICS and IMS/TM. For CICS, you would choose to only protect ENTRY threads for high-volume transactions and couple that with the use of packages bound with the BIND option RELEASE(DEALLOCATE) for frequently executed packages. Allow the rest of the transactions to run as POOL threads. When a transaction runs on POOL threads, it is normally a moot point as to whether the packages running on the POOL thread are bound using the BIND option RELEASE(COMMIT|DEALLOCATE). There is normally no thread reuse in the pool, and BIND option RELEASE(DEALLOCATE) will bring no benefit unless thread reuse can be achieved.

For DRDA workloads, do not overuse BIND option RELEASE(DEALLOCATE) on packages, because it will drive up the MAXDBAT requirement.

Another point to remember with all of the DB2 attachment packages is that there is a tradeoff when you use persistent threads with packages with RELEASE(DEALLOCATE). Doing so will impact BIND/REBIND and SQL DDL concurrency. When you have a high-volume transaction that justifies use of persistent threads running with packages bound with RELEASE(DEALLOCATE), then BIND/REBIND and DDL activity cannot break in.

Many customers fail to see the benefit of thread reuse and avoiding the repetitive cost of thread create and thread terminate per transaction. Here is the explanation as it relates to CICS: If you are incurring the overhead of thread create and terminate, you cannot see the overhead in the DB2 accounting record. On the other hand, if you avoid the overhead of thread create and terminate, you also cannot see the overhead saved in the DB2 accounting record.

CICS uses the L8 TCB to process DB2 work, regardless of whether the application is running as thread safe or not. The CPU time associated with thread create and terminate (or the avoidance thereof) shows up in the CICS System Management Facility (SMF) Record Type 110 record. Note that before the introduction of the Open Transaction Environment (OTE) in CICS, CICS did not even capture the cost of thread create and terminate in the SMF Record Type 110 record. The CPU cost of thread create and terminate was not captured. Provided successful thread reuse is achieved, the benefit of running with packages on the thread bound with the BIND option RELEASE(DEALLOCATE) will show up in a reduction in the Class 2 TCB Time in the DB2 Accounting Record (SMF Record Type 101).

For some customer installations, DB2 10 for z/OS also has the potential to reduce the number of DB2 members in a data sharing group. Some customers had to grow their DB2 processing capacity horizontally due to the 31-bit virtual storage constraint in the DBM1 address space by growing the width of the data sharing group by adding additional DB2 members to absorb the total workload and requirement for threads. Some of these same customer installations added new LPARs to support the additional DB2 members. Other customer installations decided to run multiple members from the same DB2 sharing group on the existing LPARs.

Why? The customer installations wanted to limit the number of LPARs running on the faster z10 and z196 systems because of increasing LPAR overheads. This could be achieved by running the existing number of DB2 members over a smaller number of LPARs (i.e., now run multiple DB2 members on the now smaller number of LPARs). However, if additional DB2 members were required to provide increased thread processing capacity, the installation could spread the additional DB2 members across the existing LPARs (i.e., now multiple DB2 members running on each LPAR).

Now, with the generous DBM1 31-bit virtual storage constraint relief in DB2 10 for z/OS, such customers have the ability to reduce the total number of DB2 members in a data sharing group. This change can reduce the number of DB2 members from the same data sharing group running on the same LPAR down to one, and it can possibly lead to a reduction in the total number of LPARs as well. The ability to reduce the total number of DB2 members and/or the number of LPARs will provide further price/performance (cost reduction) improvements.

Before you consolidate DB2 members and LPARs, there are some potential issues to consider. For example, what will happen to the logging rate when you push more workload through a single DB2 subsystem? By running more workload through an individual DB2 subsystem, you will drive up the aggregate logging rate for that DB2 subsystem. Can the size of the active log configuration, the dataset placement, and the I/O subsystem cope with the load? Will output log buffer latch contention be aggravated?

You also need to consider the increase in SMF data volume generated per LPAR. In DB2 10 for z/OS, you can now enable DB2 compression of instrumentation record data written to SMF (e.g., DB2 accounting trace data) to reduce the SMF data volume generated. DB2 instrumentation data, such as statistics trace and accounting trace records, are typically written out to SMF and can benefit from this enhancement.

A new DB2 system parameter (ZPARM) called SMFCOMP, once enabled by setting to YES, turns on DB2 compression of the output records written to SMF. This compression applies to any instrumentation record, not just statistics and accounting, that is written out to the SMF destination. We have observed up to a 70 percent reduction in the volume of SMF data generated when the SMF compression in DB2 is turned on. The CPU overhead incurred is only about 1 percent—representing a very good tradeoff.

This enhancement provides an opportunity for improved problem determination (PD) and problem source identification (PSI) by offering the possibility of turning off the use of accounting roll-up for DDF and Recovery Resource Services attachment facility (RRSAF) workloads (default). We introduced this support in DB2 for z/OS Version 8 to reduce SMF data volume, but one of the drawbacks of accounting roll-up was that it compromised the PD/PSI of performance problems.

By rolling up the transaction activity for multiple transactions into a single accounting record, you will lose information about the outlying, badly performing transactions. The information about the poor performance of the outlying transactions gets "amortized" away by the accounting roll-up. Given the introduction of SMF data compression in DB2 10 for z/OS, SMF compression may be a better option to control SMF data volume than using the accounting roll-up.

Another consideration when migrating to any new DB2 for z/OS release is the impact of increased dump size due to growth in the total DB2 working set size (and the need to avoid partial dump capture). DB2 10 for z/OS is no different. Partial dump capture can seriously compromise the PD/PSI performed by DB2 for z/OS Development. Prevailing production experience with DB2 10 for z/OS is that MAXSPACE(DUMPSRV) should be set to at least 16 GB to avoid a partial dump. Customer installations should make sure sufficient real storage is provisioned on the LPAR for the increased MAXSPACE(DUMPSRV) requirement and avoid the system spilling out into auxiliary storage. It is vitally important to capture a dump very quickly in a small number of seconds to avoid disruption on the subject LPAR and sympathy sickness spreading to the rest of the data sharing.

Finally, we want to re-emphasize the continued business and technical value of DB2 data sharing to differentiate the z/OS platform in terms of providing continuous availability by masking *both planned and unplanned* outages. You want to avoid large single points of failure. For example, consider a recommended minimum configuration of four-way data sharing for true, continuous availability, assuming a two processor (CEC) configuration.

By "four-way data sharing," we mean that you have two boxes (CECs) and there are two LPARs running on each box (a total of four LPARs). A single DB2 member would run on each LPAR. That is the recommended minimum recommendation for true, continuous availability and to maintain performance, if you want to maintain your service level agreement (SLA). In this four-way configuration, if you were to lose a DB2 member or one LPAR, the surviving DB2 member on the alternate LPAR running on the same box can take on 100 percent of the workload and use all the CPU processing capacity available on the box (CEC).

Planning for real storage

Let us discuss now, in more detail, the need to carefully plan, provision, and monitor real storage consumption. Most DB2 9 for z/OS and DB2 for z/OS Version 8 customers are properly configured and provisioned in terms of real storage. However, some are running so low on available real storage that part of the DB2 working set is often being paged out, intermittently, to auxiliary (DASD) storage.

Worse still, if a dump were to be taken on the system at the wrong time, the dump capture would take several minutes instead of a few seconds to complete, and it could spread sympathy sickness around a data sharing group. Information about real and auxiliary frames used is already recorded in the IFCID 225 record generated by DB2 for z/OS. However, although the provided information has been improved, with more details recorded in DB2 10 for z/OS, the information previously furnished in IFCID 225 has not allowed a customer installation to effectively monitor 64-bit shared and 64-bit common storage when running multiple DB2 subsystems on the same LPAR.

A new DB2 APAR, PM24723, for DB2 10 for z/OS provides the needed capability. The new APAR uses the enhanced capability provided with MVS™ APAR OA35885, which provides a new callable service to Real Storage Manager (RSM) to report REAL and AUX usage for a given addressing range for shared objects. APAR PM24723 will have this new MVS APAR as a prerequisite. The PTFs for DB2 APAR PM24723 and MVS APAR OA35885 can be applied independently.

The other advantage is that this same DB2 APAR provides a much-needed real storage management DISCARD function within DB2 when available real storage is overcommitted and the MVS system starts to make very significant use of auxiliary storage.

Some customers have used a hidden DB2 system parameter called SPRMRSMX (real storage "kill switch") when running multiple DB2 subsystems on the same LPAR. The SPRMRSMX ZPARM protects individual DB2 subsystems and other subsystems running on the LPAR such that if one of the DB2 subsystems were to "run away" in terms of virtual storage use, that subsystem would be "sacrificed" so that the other DB2 subsystems running on the same LPAR could continue to run.

Customers using system parameter SPRMRSMX are strongly recommended to carefully estimate and then set the value. If the value set is too small, there will be false positives and DB2 subsystems will be sacrificed unnecessarily. If the value is set too high, the LPAR (and all the DB2 subsystems running on it) will die before the runaway DB2 subsystem is detected and sacrificed. The "normal" working set size of a DB2 subsystem needs to be determined based on IFCID 225 record data; this value should then be uplifted by a certain factor to provide for contingency. The resulting value should be used as the SPRMRSMX setting. The factor applied to determine the final value for SPRMRSMX will typically be around 1.2X to 1.5X for a production DB2 subsystem. This factor may need to be increased to 2X if the DB2 subsystem has small buffer pools. DB2 9 for z/OS and DB2 for z/OS Version 8 customers who are currently using this system parameter will need to carefully re-evaluate the value set when migrating to DB2 10 for z/OS. In DB2 10 for z/OS, the hidden system parameter SPRMRSMX is replaced by an opaque system parameter called REALSTORAGE_MAX.

In DB2 10 for z/OS, you will need to factor in the increased use of 64-bit shared private and common storage to establish the new DB2 for z/OS storage footprint. IPL amounts for the LPAR will need to be adjusted based on the number of DB2 members running on that LPAR. The following values are on a "per DB2 subsystem" basis (i.e., you would double them when running two DB2 subsystems on an LPAR, triple them for three, etc.):

Storage area	IPL amount
64-bit private	1 TB
64-bit shared	128 GB
64-bit common	6 GB

Note carefully that these values are not indicative of real storage to be used, or even of virtual storage to be allocated; they simply represent reserving an addressing range for DB2 for z/OS to use. These large memory object areas are allocated above the 2 GB bar, and they will be sparsely populated. Virtual storage is not allocated until the pieces of storage are actually referenced.

INSERT performance

INSERT is one of the most important SQL statements in DB2 for z/OS. It is also one of the most challenging for any database management system (DBMS) to handle. It represents a tradeoff between optimizing performance in terms of maximizing throughput (inserts per second) and minimizing contention versus efficient space reuse. Previous DB2 for z/OS releases have focused on improving INSERT performance. DB2 10 for z/OS provides some improvements for all table space types. There was particular focus on improving INSERT performance for universal table spaces, both partition by range (PBR) and partition by growth (PBG).

Over the longer term, what we want to do in DB2 for z/OS is converge all the classic table space types to be UTS and deprecate the old, classic table space types. DB2 10 for z/OS includes two specific enhancements to improve insert performance for UTS. First, UTS now supports MEMBER CLUSTER to help where there is excessive page latch and page p-lock contention on space map pages and on data pages when using row-level locking. Second, changes were made to the space search algorithm, making the algorithm used by UTS now more like that used by the classic partitioned table space.

The performance goal for INSERT in DB2 10 for z/OS was for UTS to be equal to, or better than, the classic partitioned table space. While we are not there yet, the performance is dramatically improved. However, the improvement relative to DB2 9 for z/OS is very workload dependent. There is still a tradeoff between maximizing throughput and minimizing contention versus efficient space reuse. We still have some work to do on UTS, in the area of both PBR/PBG when using row-level locking and where the insert activity is sequential.

Three specific improvements to INSERT in DB2 10 for z/OS should help all table space types. The first is to reduce log record sequence number (LRSN) spin for inserts to the same index or data page. As processors become faster, such as z10 and z196, there is an increased possibility of duplicate LRSN values occuring and spins having to occur. When a spin occurs, processing loops in the DB2 code take place waiting for the LRSN value to change. The LRSN value is used in data sharing to serialize restart/recovery actions, and it is the high-order six bytes of the store clock (STCK) value. The LRSN is incremented every 16 microseconds. As processors get faster, there is increased potential for duplicate LRSN values to occur and the need to spin. We already made some improvements in DB2 9 for z/OS and DB2 for z/OS Version 8 regarding this issue.

In DB2 10 for z/OS, when we have multi-row inserts (MRI) or single simple inserts within an application processing loop, we avoid the LRSN spins for the same page that would have occurred previously. The results have been very impressive. This improvement applies when you use multi-row inserts to the same page or have simple inserts within an application processing loop to the same page, in a data sharing environment.

The second improvement, which works very well, is an optimization for "pocket" sequential insert activity. This is where you have multiple "hot spots" in the key range and the INSERTs are "piling in" on these hot spots. During insert, DB2 Index Manager (IM) identifies to the DB2 Data Manager (DM) the candidate RID value (page) to be used to place the new data row. DB2 Index Manager now returns the next-lowest key RID value. The end result achieved is a much better chance to find the space and avoid a space search.

The third improvement relates to parallel index read I/O, which works very well and is best-suited when it is activated where there are random index key inserts. This mechanism is normally enabled when three or more indices exist on the table and you are performing random index key INSERTs. It can also be enabled when only two indices exist on the table and the table is defined with the MEMBER CLUSTER option and/or APPEND option. Previously, you would see a lot of random sync page read I/O. We now do parallel index read I/O when there are three or more indices on the table, or two indices when the table is defined with MEMBER CLUSTER and/or APPEND options. This improves throughput by taking the synchronous read I/O delay activity out of the elapsed time for each insert.

To compensate elsewhere for the potential increase in CPU resource consumption as a result of parallel index read I/O during insert, DB2 now makes the CPU resource consumption associated with prefetch engines (sequential prefetch, list prefetch, and limit prefetch) and with deferred write engines eligible for System z9® Integrated Information Processor (zIIP) offload. These types of processing are now offloaded to zIIP processors to compensate for any possible increase in CPU resource consumption when performing parallel index read I/O for random key INSERTs.

Accounting Trace Class 3 enhancement

In DB2 10 for z/OS, there are now separate counters for IRLM Lock/Latch Wait and DB2 Latch Wait events in the DB2 accounting trace Class 3 accounting. Previously, both types of wait events were included in a single counter. When analyzing application performance problems, you had to try to figure out which type of wait activity was causing the value of this single counter to be elevated.

The next improvement relates to data sharing. One of the disadvantages of having very large, local buffer pools with many group buffer pool (GBP) dependent objects, was that DB2 for z/OS used to scan the local buffer pool for each GBP-dependent object during DB2 shutdown. These scans potentially added a lot of delay in shutting down the DB2 subsystem. DB2 also used to scan the local buffer pool when an object went into or out of GBP dependency. This activity could add a lot of overhead, depending on how often these transitions were made.

In DB2 10 for z/OS, we expect faster DB2 shutdown times because we avoid the local buffer pool scan per GBP-dependent object during the shutdown. We now also avoid the local buffer pool scan when an individual object (pageset/partition) transitions into or out of GBP dependency.

Inline LOB column values are now supported in DB2 10 for z/OS. The size of the inline portion can be specified as a system parameter (ZPARM) or on an individual object basis. There is no "one size fits all" value for the use of inline LOBs. So, using a general value as a system parameter is unlikely to be a good choice as design default.

You will get more value by setting the inline LOB value on the SQL DDL for the specific object. The performance tuning goal is to avoid access to the auxiliary table space for the majority of LOB column values. This function is aimed primarily at applications that have many, small LOB column values (i.e., up to a few hundred bytes in length, although they could be several thousand bytes in length).

The design goal for the inline LOB value is to store the complete column value inline, in the base table row, and avoid access altogether to the auxiliary table space. The potential exists for significant CPU resource consumption reduction and elapsed time improvement if this can be achieved by setting the right value for the size of the inline portion.

However, if you store all (or part) of the LOB column value inline, in the base table row, and then very rarely reference the LOB column value, you may impact performance elsewhere because you will get fewer rows per page. In any event, you may need to consider increasing the page size for the table space.

In the worst case, if you have made a poor choice for the inline LOB column value, you will have the first part of most LOB column values in the base table and the remaining part of each LOB column value in the auxiliary table space. So, not only will you get no benefit, but you will actually increase CPU overhead and waste DASD space. But another advantage to inline LOB column values is that the portion of the LOB column value that is stored in the base table row is now eligible for data compression and can be used in index on expression.

Another performance enhancement to DB2 10 for z/OS relates to active log writes. Before DB2 10 for z/OS, DB2 active log writes were always done serially to log copy 1 and log copy 2 when rewriting a previously written log CI that was partially filled. DB2 would write to log copy 1, wait, and then, when it was successful, write to log copy 2. The reason for this was that, prior to RAID devices, we had single, large, expensive disks (SLEDs). We were always concerned that, when we rewrote a previously partially filled log CI, we might destroy the previous version of the log CI and its contents.

With the increased reliability provided by RAID devices, there is no longer any reason to perform rewrites of log CIs serially. DB2 10 for z/OS now always performs active log writes in parallel. This enhancement can generate significant elapsed time improvements for applications that commit frequently or when other forced writes occur (e.g., related to index leaf page splits).

Hash access vs. index-only access

Hash access basically "competes" with clustered index access, and specifically with index-only access combined with index lookaside. In an effort to reduce CPU resource consumption, hash access tries to avoid going through an index B-tree structure with many levels to access the data row to improve query performance. The advantage that clustered index access has is that DB2 tries to maintain clustered data row access. Index-only access avoids access to the data row completely. DB2 10 for z/OS also provides the opportunity to have a unique index with INCLUDE columns.

Today, you may have multiple indices on a table. One index is there to enforce the uniqueness of the primary key. You may have added another index to improve performance (e.g., better filtering, avoiding sort). The leading columns may be the same in both indices. You may now include additional columns in a unique index and still use that same index as before to enforce the unique constraint.

The length of each index entry will be larger. Now, the advantage of a unique index with INCLUDE columns is that it gives you the ability to satisfy the unique constraint check *and* provide the performance benefits you want for query. The result is that you can reduce the number of indexes required for performance reasons. For every index you can avoid, you will improve the performance of INSERT and DELETE and possibly improve UPDATE performance, as well.

A number of customers evaluated both methods to try to find the "sweet spot." There is definite value from hash access, provided you can determine that sweet spot. However, in practice, the sweet spot has proved to be relatively small. Here are guidelines for identifying the sweet spot:

- High NLEVELS in index (more than two)
- Access by applications needs to be purely direct row access by primary key
- Truly random access
- Read-intensive, not volatile
- No range queries (minimize BETWEENs, >, <, and so on)
- Many rows per page

One of the key points about hash access performance is that you want to "tune" the space allocation of the fixed-sized hash area so that you reduce the number of rows that go into the overflow index (i.e., control overflow). If the primary fixed hash area is too small, you will have many rows in the overflow index; on the other hand, if the primary area is too large, you will have too much random I/O. It is important to minimize or avoid altogether rows in the overflow index.

To help with sizing the fixed hash area size, DB2 10 for z/OS provides a new option on the REORG utility called AUTOESTSPACE(YES). When you perform REORG with this option, it uses information from Real Time Statistics (RTS) to resize the primary fixed hash area and reduce the number of rows in the overflow index. However, even after such a REORG, there may still be some small number of data rows in the overflow index.

Finally, when you migrate to hash access, you will see some degradation in the elapsed time for both LOAD and REORG utility executions.

Availability

DB2 10 for z/OS provides a number of enhancements to reduce planned outages for applications and improve the success of the online REORG utility.

Online schema evolution

"Deferred Alter" is a new feature in DB2 10 for z/OS. With this mechanism, when you make a schema change, the change goes "pending" and it is stored in the DB2 catalog. The next time you perform an online REORG, the online REORG will materialize the pending changes. You can set up many Deferred Alters. Each of the changes will go pending in the DB2 catalog until the subsequent online REORG occurs, when the changes will be materialized.

Why is this feature important? The Deferred Alter mechanism now gives you a migration path away from the classic table space types of simple, segmented, and partitioned—which contain a single table—over to universal table spaces.

Note

UTS is a prerequisite for some of the new DB2 10 for z/OS functions, such as hash access, inline LOB, and currently committed. It is also a prerequisite for the cloned table function in DB2 9 for z/OS. If a table space is a simple table space or a segmented table space, you can have only one table per table space to be able to use this migration path to UTS, because UTS still only supports one table per table space.

Note

This migration path to UTS is a "one-way ticket" only. Once you migrate to UTS, you cannot go back using the same Deferred Alter mechanism to simple, segmented, or partitioned table spaces. To return to using the classic table space types, you would have to unload the data, drop the table space, redefine the table space as it was before, and reload the data.

Note also that point-in-time recovery to a point *before* a successful materializing online REORG is not possible. If, for example, you have incorrect results from REORG, possibly because the wrong rows were discarded or an application change needs to be rolled back, you cannot recover to a point in time before the online REORG.

Now, once you have migrated to UTS PBG/PBR, you can change attributes such as DSSIZE and index page size. You can turn MEMBER CLUSTER on and off or migrate to and from hash access. These abilities are all provided by the Deferred Alter mechanism, followed by the online REORG. This function works very well and can help reduce the number of destructive database changes that previously caused database down time and impacted the availability of dependent critical business applications.

To summarize, the benefits of Deferred Alter are:

✓ Streamlining the move to UTS
✓ Reducing the administrative time and cost associated with moving to UTS
✓ Helping to minimize errors
✓ Reducing outages

Another new option is the FORCE option of online REORG. In the last part of the

REORG, when you are in the final attempt to drain the object and are about to make the switch, if there are "active" threads blocking, the FORCE option allows DB2 10 for z/OS to kill the active threads.

Early beta customers found limited value to this function because if the threads were active in DB2, DB2 would cancel the threads (good). But if the threads were inactive, the FORCE function did not kill them, and the online REORG failed. Then, when the inactive threads became active after the online REORG failed, the threads were canceled on their way back in. So the FORCE option is not a guaranteed way to kill all blocking threads and allow the online REORG to always make the switch.

Also new with DB2 10 for z/OS, the online REORG of LOB table spaces provides a DISCARD option. Early customers thought this feature was of limited value because it cannot handle LOB column values greater than 32K bytes.

Other Issues

First, there is the retained ability to create classic partitioned table spaces (PTSs). In DB2 10 for z/OS, the classic PTS is now deprecated, meaning that, by default, you will not be able to create any new classic PTS. An attempt will be made to honor the request by creating a UTS PBR. However, a CREATE of UTS will support only the table-based controlled partitioning syntax. The legacy, index-based control partitioning syntax is not supported for UTS.

So, by default, you may not be able to create any new, classic PTS. However, customers demanded the continued ability to create classic PTSs because there are still a few areas where classic PTS has value over UTS. The good news is that you can still create classic PTSs in DB2 10 for z/OS, and these table spaces are still officially supported. There are two ways to continue to create classic PTSs:

1. Specify SEGSIZE=0 on the CREATE TABLESPACE statement.
2. Set new system parameter DPSEGSZ to zero (the default is 32).

Either of these methods will let you create classic PTSs in DB2 10 for z/OS.

For customers who still have old COBOL and PL/1 programs, the DB2 for OS/390® Version 7 lookalike precompiler (DSNHPC7) for COBOL and PL/I is *still* provided in DB2 10 for z/OS.

The concurrency issues with parallel SQL DDL execution are not absolutely solved in DB2 10 for z/OS, despite the DB2 catalog restructure in Enable New Function Mode (ENFM). While the restructure was eventually successful to allow for parallel BIND/REBIND activity, most customers still experience deadlocks when running parallel jobs with heavy SQL DDL against different databases within the same commit scope. Therefore, some customers will still have to run their SQL DDL jobs single-threaded.

BIND/REBIND issues

With single-thread BIND/REBIND, early customers have reported degraded CPU and elapsed time performance on entry into DB2 10 for z/OS CM. There are two reasons for this experience:

* PLANMGMT is now ON by default, and its default value is EXTENDED.
* New indexes defined for post-ENFM processing, when hash links are eliminated, are being used even in CM.

Because we have a single code path (no dual path processing) across the different modes (CM, ENFM, NFM) of DB2 10 for z/OS, those indices are now used even in Conversion Mode. For most customers, single-thread BIND/REBIND performance remains important because there are no concurrency improvements until after the DB2 catalog restructure is completed at the end of ENFM.

With parallel BIND/REBIND jobs, particularly in data sharing mode, we identified and addressed a number of concurrency and performance problems prior to general availability, including performance problems related to the repetitive DELETE/INSERT processing.

A number of customers have reported problems related to significant space growth in the SPT01 table space and in the associated LOB table spaces (SYSSPUXA, SYSSPUXB). The problem happens when an old READLRSN exists on the object. The problem can be observed in both data sharing and non-data sharing systems. Frequent reorganizations of these table spaces have been required to reclaim the excessive DASD space usage. This solution has been unacceptable to some of these customers. APAR PM64226 has now been opened to address the space growth issue associated with the LOB table spaces only. The solution involves being more aggressive on space reuse within the same DB2 subsystem or member. This excessive space growth has been observed for other LOB table spaces within the DB2 catalog and directory (e.g., SYSDBDXA). The subject APAR will address the excessive space growth for these LOB table space objects as well. The problem related to excessive space use in the base SPT01 table space is still being worked through.

The concurrency of parallel BIND/REBIND jobs is now working well after the ENFM processing is complete, even across different members of the same data sharing group. Several relevant fixing APARs must be applied to make this happen:

APAR	Description
PM24721	Inefficient space search for out-of-line LOB in data sharing
PM27073	Inline LOB with compression for SPT01 to address SPT01
PM27973	More efficient space reuse for base table and UTS

With these APARs applied, concurrent BIND/REBIND activity in both data sharing and non-data sharing systems works very well after you get past the ENFM processing.

Once beyond ENFM processing, we recommend that customers change existing procedures to run BIND/REBIND activity in parallel (but you should not do this until after ENFM). Doing so gives customer installations the opportunity to get back to and improve upon the elapsed time performance (throughput) levels experienced in DB2 9 for z/OS and DB2 for z/OS Version 8 and to reduce application downtime when implementing new enterprise application releases.

Incompatible Changes

The most important incompatibility relates to the use of the CHAR(decimal), VARCHAR(decimal), CAST(decimal AS CHAR), and CAST(decimal AS VARCHAR) built-in functions. As an application programmer, you may have used one of these functions and applied it against a decimal column value to pull out a numeric value to assign to particular fields.

The incompatible change is documented in the *DB2 10 for z/OS Installation and Migration Guide* (GC19-2974). The challenge for customers is how to identify the rogue applications that are exposed to the incompatible changes and need to be corrected. How do you identify what the exposure is?

By working with customers in the beta program, we were able to identify the issue related to the CHAR(decimal) built-in function. APAR PM29124 was created to restore the compatible behavior of pre–DB2 10 for z/OS releases, by default, for the CHAR(decimal) built-in function. This support applied only to the CHAR(decimal) function. The subject APAR introduced a new DB2 system parameter called BIF_COMPATIBILITY. The options for BIF_COMPATIBILITY are V9 and CURRENT to enable and disable it, respectively. The parameter's default value of V9 continues to allow the old behavior for the CHAR(decimal) function, but even with this setting you still get the new incompatible DB2 10 for z/OS behavior for VARCHAR/CAST(decimal) functions. A new IFCID 366 was made available under DB2 10 for z/OS to enable customers to trace and identify programs potentially at risk that require investigation and correction. This IFCID 366 trace record covers both static and dynamic SQL. IFCID 366 support was also made available under DB2 9 for z/OS as a USERMOD on request. APAR PM70455 has now been opened to formally retrofit IFCID 366 back to DB2 9 for z/OS.

APAR PM66095 has now been opened; this APAR increases the scope of the DB2 subsystem parameter BIF_COMPATIBILITY to include VARCHAR(decimal), CAST(decimal AS CHAR), and CAST(decimal AS VARCHAR) built in functions. It also adds a third option, V9_DECIMAL_VARCHAR. These settings allow you to specify whether:

- The current DB2 10 for z/OS release format should be returned by all of these functions (BIF_COMPATIBILITY=CURRENT)
- The DB2 9 for z/OS format should be returned by all of these functions (BIF_COMPATIBILITY=V9_DECIMAL_VARCHAR)

- The current release format should be used by all of these functions except the CHAR(decimal) function, which should return the DB2 9 for z/OS format (BIF_COMPATIBILITY=V9)

The next incompatibility issue is with SQL stored procedures. If you have a native SQL procedure that was implemented and/or regenerated under DB2 10 for z/OS and you need to fall back to DB2 9 for z/OS, that native SQL procedure will not run. The workaround is to run the **ALTER PROCEDURE REGENERATE** statement on the DB2 9 for z/OS member. APAR PM13525 will deal with this issue automatically for you.

Finally, there is an issue with the **CREATE TRIGGER** statement for triggers created on DB2 10 for z/OS. If you fall back to DB2 9 for z/OS, such triggers won't work. The workaround: Drop and re-create these triggers under DB2 9 for z/OS after fallback.

Migration and Planning Considerations

This section reviews key migration and planning considerations in planning for DB2 10 for z/OS.

Migration strategy

As in previous releases, we recommend a short time for mixed-release coexistence in data sharing. A short period for Enable New Function Mode is also highly recommended. Support from vendors may affect the staging of the migration. One consideration for Conversion Mode is that some of the new performance improvements cannot be used.

There are options to consider that will affect the timing of when to move from Test to QA to Production. Even though there are better controls for preventing the use of new SQL functions, it is advisable not to have a long time gap when Test and Production levels are at different releases and at different maintenance levels for the same release. You now have more granularity in the migration process and can move through mode by mode. Some customers migrate both Test and Production to CM, wait and stabilize for a while, and then migrate to New Function Mode (NFM) through ENFM in a very short time.

The chart shown in Figure 1.3 summarizes the history of DB2 releases. The top line tracks the year when each release became generally available (GA). The arrows show that the only releases where it was possible to skip a release were from DB2 for OS/390 Version 5 to DB2 for OS/390 Version 7 and from DB2 for z/OS Version 8 to DB2 10 for z/OS.

The lower part of the chart indicates the steps within the upgrade path from DB2 for z/OS Version 8 or DB2 9 for z/OS to DB2 10 for z/OS. The double-headed arrows indicate where you can "go back" a step, if necessary.

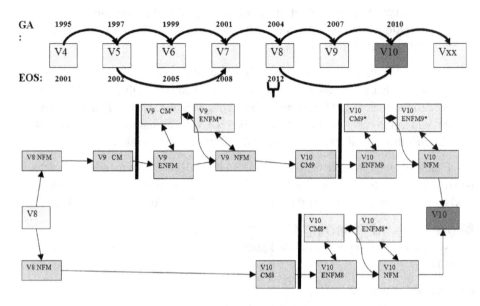

Figure 1.3: Timeline of DB2 releases and upgrade paths

Note

If you are migrating from DB2 for z/OS Version 8, you have a decision to make. Should you go to DB2 9 for z/OS, or skip it and go directly to DB2 10 for z/OS? Once you decide to migrate to DB2 10 for z/OS CM8, you can still return to DB2 for z/OS V8 by falling back. But you *cannot* then try later to migrate forward to DB2 9 for z/OS CM.

Planning considerations

In general, the DB2 10 for z/OS migration process is very similar to that for both DB2 for z/OS Version 8 and DB2 9 for z/OS. It works well, with few customers experiencing problems with migration and fallback. The ENFM process in DB2 10 for z/OS runs a lot longer than it did for DB2 9 for z/OS and even longer than it did on DB2 for z/OS Version 8.

You can migrate to DB2 10 for z/OS CM from either DB2 for z/OS Version 8 NFM or DB2 9 for z/OS NFM. You cannot migrate through either of the following two scenarios:

- Once you migrate forward from DB2 for z/OS Version 8 NFM to DB2 10 for z/OS CM8, you can always fall back to DB2 for z/OS Version 8 NFM, but you *cannot* then migrate forward to DB2 9 for z/OS CM.
- Once you migrate forward from DB2 for z/OS Version 8 NFM to DB2 9 for z/OS CM, you can always fall back to DB2 for z/OS Version 8 NFM, but you *cannot* then migrate forward to DB2 10 for z/OS CM8.

Online migration in 24x7 environments

Increasingly, customers are asking whether they can run jobs DSNTIJTC (the CATMAINT utility) and DSNTIJEN alongside critical business application services. It is technically possible to run these jobs alongside well-behaved online transaction workloads. DSNTIJTC and DSNTIJEN use SQL DDL with frequent commit and REORG SHRLEVEL(REFERENCE). The jobs are designed to fail gracefully, leaving the DB2 catalog and directory fully operational. After problem determination is complete, the respective failing job can be corrected and resubmitted. The respective failing job will then restart from where it left off. However, there are some "rules of the game," and you must be prepared to play by the rules. Jobs DSNTIJTC and DSNTIJEN should be scheduled during a relatively quiet period. In a non-data sharing system, you must stop all application workloads when the DSNTIJTC job is running. In a data sharing system, you must route work away from the DB2 member where the DSNTIJTC job is running by temporarily changing workload balancing and sysplex routing schemes.

You should also synthetically stop all of the following workload types from running: SQL DDL, GRANTs and REVOKEs, BIND/REBIND, utilities, and monitors. All essential business-critical workloads that are running should commit frequently. You must be prepared to watch and intervene if needed. There is a strong recommendation to perform pre-migration catalog migration testing. You must be prepared for the DSNTIJTC job and/or the DSNTIJEN job to possibly fail or for some business transactions to fail.

There is also some critical maintenance you should apply. APAR PM62572 deals with undetected deadlock contention failure during the switch phase of the ENFM REORG step. APAR PM58575 avoids auto-bind triggering deadlock with RTS.

If, as a customer installation, you are not prepared to play by these rules of the game, then take the outage, quiescing all applications, and run the DSNTIJTC or DSNTIJEN job with the migrating DB2 member started with ACCESS(MAINT).

Here are some important APARs to remember:

- Fallback Toleration SPE:
  ◦ APAR PK56922

- Early Code for DB2 V8/V9:
  ◦ APAR PK87280 (supersedes APAR PK61766)

- Information APARs:
  ◦ II14474: V8 to V10
  ◦ II14477: V9 to V10

If you are migrating from DB2 for z/OS Version 8 NFM, the bootstrap data set (BSDS) must be reformatted for the larger number of active/archive log tracking.

For those who operate DB2 Connect™, the recommended minimum level to support DB2 10 for z/OS is now DB2 Connect V9.5 FP7. At least DB2 Connect V9.7 FP3A is required to support the new functions of DB2 10 for z/OS.

Deprecated DB2 system parameters (ZPARMs)

As with every release of DB2 for z/OS, DB2 for z/OS provides a list of system parameters slated for deprecation in DB2 10 for z/OS. Several customers have, however, misunderstood the term "deprecation" to imply that the system parameter has been removed or is rendered meaningless in the current release. The real meaning of deprecation in this context is that the system parameter is still active in the current release but has been identified as being removed in a future release.

The wording in the *DB2 10 for z/OS Installation and Migration Guide* has been clarified and now states that although the deprecated system parameters are supported in DB2 10 for z/OS, they will be removed in a later release of DB2 for z/OS.

Table 1.2 summarizes the deprecated system parameters and their behavior after DB2 10 for z/OS.

Deprecated system parameter	Behavior in releases after DB2 10 for z/OS
DISABSCL	In later DB2 releases, subsystems behave as if DISABSCL is set to NO.
DPSEGSZ	In later DB2 releases, subsystems behave as if DPSEGSZ is set to 32.
OJPERFEH	In later DB2 releases, subsystems behave as if OJPERFEH is set to YES.
OPTIOWGT	In later DB2 releases, subsystems behave as if OPTIOWGT is set to ENABLE.
OPTIXIO	In later DB2 releases, subsystems behave as if OPTIXIO is set to ON.
PTCDIO	In later DB2 releases, subsystems behave as if PTCDIO is set to OFF.
RETVLCFK	In later DB2 releases, subsystems behave as if RETVLCFK is set to NO. Use of non-padded indexes is recommended.
SEQCACH	In later DB2 releases, subsystems behave as if SEQCACH is set to SEQ.
SEQPRES	In later DB2 releases, subsystems behave as if SEQPRES is set to YES.
SMSDCFL	In later DB2 releases, the CREATE STOGROUP and ALTER STOGROUP statements have been enhanced to include SMS data class parameters.
SMSDCIX	In later DB2 releases, the CREATE STOGROUP and ALTER STOGROUP statements have been enhanced to include SMS data class parameters.
STATCLUS	In later DB2 release, subsystems behave as if STATCLUS is set to ENHANCED.

Table 1.2: System parameters deprecated in DB2 10 for z/OS

Despite the clarification in the documentation, there is still concern that an important optimizer-related system parameter, OPTIOWGT, could be incorrectly set by some customers because it is listed as deprecated. There is a recommendation for OPTIOWGT to be set to ENABLE, the default value. As from DB2 9 for z/OS and later, there is a very strong recommendation from DB2 for z/OS Development for customers to use the default. A new APAR, PM70046, has been released for DB2 10 for z/OS to absolutely ensure that all customers follow this recommendation: Set system parameter OPTIOWGT to ENABLE to alleviate performance issues. This ZPARM will be removed in the next release of DB2.

Elimination of DDF Private Protocol

Many customers are still using DDF Private Protocol under DB2 for z/OS Version 8 and DB2 9 for z/OS. Use of DDF Private Protocol in DB2 10 for z/OS is definitely not supported. *There is zero tolerance for the use of DDF Private Protocol in DB2 10 for z/OS.* You must absolutely eliminate all use of DDF Private Protocol before starting DB2 10 for z/OS in CM.

Many customers have local plans and packages (CICS, IMS, batch, and so on) that have been accidentally mistagged as requiring the use of DDF Private Protocol. These mistagged plans and packages will be tolerated at allocation time. However, if any of these packages *really* does perform an external SQL call that uses DDF Private Protocol, the call will be prevented and the application will fail immediately.

DBRMs bound directly into plans

In DB2 10 for z/OS, database request modules (DBRMs) bound directly into plans are no longer supported. However, if any DBRMs bound into plans are found at execution time, DB2 will automatically trigger the AUTOBIND process to generate packages on first allocation after entry into DB2 10 for z/OS. We choose a standard collection name to put these packages in, but the recommended best practice is to deal with DBRMs bound directly into plans *before* migrating to DB2 10 for z/OS. Any old plans and packages bound prior to DB2 for OS/390 Version 6 will also be invalidated and go through an AUTOBIND process.

SMS management of DB2 catalog and directory datasets

During CATMAINT and ENFM processing on DB2 10 for z/OS, all the new indexes and new table spaces in the DB2 catalog and directory will be created as SMS-controlled, requiring extended addressability (EA) and extended format (EF) attributes. Some customers still do not use SMS management for the DB2 catalog and directory. Before you initially start DB2 10 for z/OS and run CATMAINT, you must have set up your environments so that any new datasets created for the DB2 catalog and directory objects are placed on SMS-managed DASD volumes.

For those of you coming from DB2 for z/OS V8, partitioned data sets extended (PDSEs)—as opposed to partitioned data sets (PDSs)—are required for the SDSNLOAD, SDSNLOD2, and ADSNLOAD libraries.

The environment created by the DSNTIJSS job is *only* for DB2 catalog and directory data sets, which *must* be SMS-controlled in DB2 10 for z/OS. Other DB2 subsystem data sets, such as logs and the BSDS, are *not* accounted for in this environment.

The DSNHDECP module supports the NEWFUN parameter, which can be set to one of the following options: V10, V9, or V8. This parameter setting provides a way of stopping both static and dynamic SQL applications from using new SQL functions.

Explain tables

Many customers are still employing old plan table formats when using EXPLAIN. DB2 10 for z/OS brings some changes in this space. First, if you have any plan tables that use a format prior to DB2 for z/OS Version 8, they will not work with EXPLAIN in DB2 10 for z/OS. The plan table format and the ASCII/EBCDIC Coded Character Set Identifier (CCSID) from previous releases are deprecated in DB2 10 for z/OS. They will fail with SQLCODE -20008. If you have plan tables in DB2 for z/OS Version 8 or DB2 9 for z/OS format, you can still use them, but they will generate a warning SQLCODE +20520, regardless of whether they use CCSID EBCDIC or UNICODE.

If you use the DB2 10 for z/OS format of the plan tables with EXPLAIN, you must use UNICODE as the CCSID value. If you try to use CCSID EBCDIC with the DB2 10 for z/OS format, you will receive the following errors:

- EXPLAIN fails with RC=8 DSNT408I SQLCODE=-878.
- BIND with EXPLAIN fails with RC=8 DSNX200I.

We recommend using the DB2 10 for z/OS extended format of the plan tables with a CCSID value of UNICODE. APAR PK85068 can help you migrate existing plan tables in DB2 for z/OS Version 8 or DB2 9 for z/OS table format over to the new DB2 10 for z/OS format with a CCSID of UNICODE.

Should you "skip" DB2 9 for z/OS?

Those who decide to migrate from DB2 for z/OS Version 8 directly to DB2 10 for z/OS, are, by definition, early adopters of the new DB2 10 for z/OS release. This is because the end of support for DB2 for z/OS Version 8 came at the end of April 2012. Quite clearly, the DB2 for z/OS Version 8 to DB2 9 for z/OS migration is the safer path to take because DB2 9 for z/OS has been in the field for almost four years and is quite stable.

Early customer adopters of DB2 10 for z/OS, whether migrating from DB2 for z/OS Version 8 or DB2 9 for z/OS, should expand their plans and take extra care to mitigate the risk of instability. This is not a statement of, nor an implication that, the DB2 10 for z/OS release has any endemic problems of instability. These same recommendations would apply to any new release of DB2 for z/OS or any other major software product.

First, you should perform application regression and stress testing to keep problems away from production. Next, plan to be proactive with regard to applying regular upgrades of preventive service within a continuous process. Plan to stay more current than two full, major preventive service maintenance drops per year. A continual process to apply regular, full, major preventive service maintenance drops, including HIPERs/ PEs, is essential and required for about a year.

We strongly recommend planning for *four major* preventive service maintenance package drops in the first year, based on the quarterly RSU. Then, you can move to two major and two minor preventive service maintenance drops as the release passes through the early adopter curve. In between these drops, be vigilant and take advantage of the Enhanced HOLDDATA on a weekly basis to find out what critical HIPER PTFs and PTFs in Error (PEs) are becoming available, and then take action based on the risk of hitting the problem in your installation and the consequences of hitting the problem.

One of the advantages of following the CST/RSU process for building preventative service packages, as opposed to following the PUT route, is that it enables you to stay current on HIPERs/PEs that have gone through more testing while at the same time letting you stay further back on non-HIPERs maintenance. This capability provides some level of protection against PTFs in Error (PEs).

Finally, you have to be able to accept some level of risk and be able to handle some "bumps in the road" during the stepped migration process.

Security considerations when removing DDF Private Protocol

As previously mentioned, there is zero tolerance in DB2 10 for z/OS for applications issuing DDF Private Protocol requests. Before migrating to DB2 10 for z/OS CM, you need to plan for and work on eliminating all use of DDF Private Protocol and converting it to DRDA before you leave DB2 for z/OS Version 8 NFM or DB2 9 for z/OS NFM. There are fundamental differences in how authorization is performed, based on which distributed access protocol you use and whether the distributed access protocols are used in combination.

Let me start with a brief recap of the differences between Private Protocol and DRDA Protocol.

Private Protocol is unique to the DB2 for z/OS requester and supports static SQL statements only. The plan owner *must* have authorization to execute all SQL requests executed on the DB2 for z/OS server. The plan owner is authenticated on the DB2 for z/OS requester and not at the DB2 for z/OS server.

Now, let us compare that with the DRDA Protocol. DRDA supports both static and dynamic SQL statements. The primary auth ID and associated secondary auth IDs must have authorization to execute both static SQL packages and dynamic SQL at the DB2 for z/OS server. The primary auth ID authenticated and secondary auth IDs are associated at the DB2 for z/OS server.

In releases prior to DB2 10 for z/OS, Private Protocol and DRDA Protocol can be used by the same application within the same commit scope. You can "mix and match." Private Protocol security semantics are used due to possible inconsistent behavior, which is dependent on how the programs are coded and executed.

But there is also a difference prior to DB2 10 for z/OS in the authorizations required by an incoming DRDA connection at the DB2 for z/OS server, depending on where the connection comes from:

- Dynamic SQL DRDA connection from DB2 Connect and/or DB2 client direct connection where the connecting user ID needs authority to run the appropriate DB2 package and authority to access the DB2 table
- Dynamic SQL DRDA connection from DB2 for z/OS requester where the connecting user ID needs authority to access the DB2 table and the originating plan owner needs authority to run the appropriate DB2 package

It is different for DB2 for z/OS requester to DB2 for z/OS server because connections were designed to use Private Protocol (PP) semantics to avoid changing auth IDs when switching from Private Protocol to DRDA Protocol.

With the disappearance of Private Protocol in DB2 10 for z/OS, DB2 for z/OS Development have decided to bring the DRDA connection from DB2 for z/OS requester to DB2 for z/OS server in line with other DRDA requesters and to change the authorizations required. This change was retrofitted back into DB2 for z/OS Version 8 and DB2 9 for z/OS with APAR PM17665. It is very important to distinguish clearly between the behavior of DRDA before and after APAR PM17665.

So things will now change with the introduction of the PTF for APAR PM17665, which applies to both DB2 for z/OS Version 8 and DB2 9 for z/OS. It provides control over the authorization checks performed when migrating from Private Protocol to DRDA Protocol. In DB2 10 for z/OS, Private Protocol security semantics are no longer used because Private Protocol has now been eliminated and DRDA Protocol has to be used for access from a DB2 for z/OS requester. Migration to V10 or the application of the PTF for APAR PM17665 does affect you even if you have everything already bound as DRDA.

After the introduction of the PTF for APAR PM17665, DB2 for z/OS Version 8 and DB2 9 for z/OS will now use DRDA authorization checks but will use the DB2 system parameter PRIVATE_PROTOCOL (previously introduced in APAR PK92339) to determine what security checks should be performed. This system parameter was introduced to allow a customer installation to prevent new use of Private Protocol after all the previous use was eliminated. To do this, a customer would set system parameter PRIVATE_PROTOCOL to NO.

So, before you disable DDF Private Protocol by setting DB2 system parameter PRIVATE_PROTOCOL to NO, ensure that all the appropriate grants are in place by granting execute privileges to any user who plans to run a package or a stored procedure package from a DB2 for z/OS requester against a DB2 for z/OS server. The requester will now be treated like any other DRDA client application running requests at a DB2 for z/OS server.

Clearly, this is a major change that could have a big impact. To help customers migrate away from Private Protocol to DRDA Protocol and handle in a timelier manner the changes introduced in security checking when the DRDA requester (client) is a DB2 for z/OS requester, both DB2 for z/OS Version 8 and DB2 9 for z/OS will provide the option to continue to prevent the introduction of new Private Protocol requests and to continue to use the Private Protocol authorization checks. The latter option is achieved by changing the setting of DB2 system parameter PRIVATE_PROTOCOL from NO to AUTH.

Save critical access paths and accounting data

BIND REPLACE and REBIND activity can cause unwanted access path changes that can lead to run time performance degradation. You should identify important queries, plans, and packages. Be sure plan tables contain access paths and costs. ALTER current plan tables to add new DB2 10 for z/OS columns. REBIND may change access paths, so extract access plan information and run REBIND with EXPLAIN under a dummy collection or a different application or program name.

Keep accounting reports for crucial queries and applications. If you have a problem and send in accounting layout long reports and the plan table data, we will be able to troubleshoot the problems more *quickly*. If you do *not* have the reports and the data, then we must *guess*.

Recommendation for REBIND under DB2 10 for z/OS

Customers understand the need to REBIND their static SQL packages to take advantage of the new query optimization enhancements. However, few customers recognize the other, potentially more important reasons why DB2 for z/OS Development suggests customers REBIND in CM on the current release.

The first reason for REBIND relates to re-creating the prior release runtime structures to be tolerated on the current release. Across a release migration, runtime optimizations such as SPROCs for fast column processing are disabled, and the prior release structures needed to be puffed up to execute on the current release. Each of these may cost several percentage points in increased CPU resource consumption without any change in access path.

Migrated packages from earlier releases also pose an increased risk of incorrect output or abend—especially the older these packages are. While DB2 for z/OS Development are diligent in their efforts to test packages created under prior releases in the current release, when you consider the number of access paths available to the DB2 for z/OS optimizer and the amount of potential maintenance under which prior REBIND might have occurred, it is virtually impossible to test all combinations. Basically, there is safety in being current on your REBINDs.

While the aforementioned reasons for REBIND are common for all releases, there are additional reasons specific to DB2 10 for z/OS. Maximizing the DBM1 31-bit virtual storage constraint relief occurs only after REBIND, as does exposure to many new runtime optimizations delivered for existing access paths, such as RID overflow to workfile or the bulk of the predicate processing improvements. Again, these optimizations are available after REBIND even if the prior access path is maintained.

Also specific to DB2 10 for z/OS: Any SQL statement that was bound prior to DB2 10 for z/OS and exploits CPU parallelism will be incrementally bound for each execution on DB2 10 for z/OS until an explicit REBIND is performed on the package. This is due to difficulty in tolerating the prior release parallelism runtime structures under DB2 10 for z/OS.

REBIND is also recommended because many of the new plan management enhancements exploit the internal access plan table representation (referred to as the Explain Data Block, or EDB) that is stored in the DB2 directory from DB2 9 for z/OS onwards.

While discussing REBIND, it is important to point out that the REBIND recommendation is for static SQL packages when migrating to CM. The vast majority of query optimization enhancements are available as soon as DB2 10 for z/OS CM, and there is no additional requirement to REBIND when migrating to NFM. Dynamic SQL is exposed to the new optimization enhancements at first execution.

Figures 1.4 and 1.5 outline the DB2 enhancements that are available without REBIND and those that require REBIND.

DB2 10 Query Performance – No REBIND Required

No REBIND required for:

- Index list prefetch INSERT index read I/O parallelism
- Workfile spanned records
- SQL PL performance
- High-performance DBATs
- Inline LOBs **(new function – requires NFM)**

Figure 1.4: DB2 10 performance enhancements available without REBIND

DB2 10 Query Performance – REBIND Required

REBIND required to take advantage of:

- Use of RELEASE(DEALLOCATE)
- Early evaluation of residual (stage 2) predicates
- IN-list improvements (new access method)
- SQL pagination (new access method)
- Query parallelism improvements
- Index include columns **(New function – requires NFM)**
- More aggressive view/table expression merge
- Predicate evaluation enhancements
- RID list overflow improvements

Figure 1.5: DB2 10 performance enhancements that require REBIND

RUNSTATS preparation before REBIND

The first step in minimizing exposure to bad access path selection is to ensure that you have a solid foundation in terms of catalog statistics. While DB2 for z/OS Development wants to provide all available optimization enhancements in CM, they also want to ensure that customers do not inadvertently REBIND on old catalog statistics if those statistics will change by default upon the first RUNSTATS collection in DB2 10 for z/OS.

The recommendation has always been to collect default RUNSTATS TABLE(ALL) INDEX(ALL) KEYCARD, and in recognition of this, the DB2 10 for z/OS default enables KEYCARD for RUNSTATS of an index—and there is no way to disable KEYCARD.

The recommendation, therefore, is to ensure that KEYCARD is being used for RUNSTATS before migration to DB2 10 for z/OS—regardless of whether the migration is from DB2 for z/OS Version 8 or from DB2 9 for z/OS.

The second important RUNSTATS change applies to customers migrating from DB2 for z/OS Version 8 to DB2 10 for z/OS. DB2 9 for z/OS introduced a significant change to the CLUSTERRATIO calculation from RUNSTATS by moving toward exploiting dynamic prefetch for index scans and data access via an index. And the RUNSTATS CLUSTERRATIO calculation has been enhanced to align with the sequential detection algorithm that triggers dynamic prefetch. This new formula is available only in CM of the release after DB2 for z/OS Version 8, meaning that DB2 9 for z/OS customers were exposed in DB2 9 for z/OS and customers migrating from DB2 for z/OS Version 8 will be first exposed in DB2 10 for z/OS CM.

For both RUNSTATS changes, it is important that you do not perform a mass REBIND in DB2 10 for z/OS CM if the next RUNSTATS execution will then change the default statistics collection. If KEYCARD is not currently used, it is recommended that you either begin using KEYCARD on RUNSTATS before migration or be prepared to run RUNSTATS before REBIND in DB2 10 for z/OS CM. Similarly, if migrating from DB2 for z/OS Version 8, run RUNSTATS before REBIND in DB2 10 for z/OS CM to pick up the new CLUSTERRATIO formula.

Data sharing customers who plan to exploit mixed-release coexistence for a short period of time with DB2 for z/OS Version 8 and DB2 10 for z/OS subsystems should consider setting system parameter STATCLUS to STANDARD while in coexistence and should avoid REBINDs where possible. When all the members of the data sharing group have been migrated to DB2 for z/OS 10 CM, it is recommended to set system parameter STATCLUS to ENHANCED (default) and to run RUNSTATS before REBIND.

Pre-production access path analysis

Some customers have copied production statistics to a pre-production environment so they could perform proactive access path analysis. Often, however, they found that environmental differences, such as CPU speed or smaller buffer pool sizes, in their pre-production environment resulted in access paths that differed from production.

To overcome the environmental differences, DB2 9 for z/OS APAR PM26475 and DB2 10 for z/OS APAR PM26973 delivered an enhancement to support overriding the environment variables. The enhancement includes two new system parameters:

- SIMULATED_CPU_SPEED
- SIMULATED_CPU_COUNT

Once set, these parameters, instead of the actual system CPU speed and number of CPs, will be used by the optimizer for access path selection. In a pre-production environment, the recommendation is to set these system parameters to match the production values.

In addition to CPU, new SYSIBM.DSN_PROFILE_ATTRIBUTES values provide the capability to override sort pool, RID pool, and buffer pool settings:

- SORT_POOL_SIZE
- MAX_RIDBLOCKS
- For buffer pools, the BP names listed in the DSNTIP1 panel—for example, 'BP8K0' corresponds to BP BP8K0

These settings impact only the information used by the optimizer and will be used in access path determination. The APAR closing text provides a more detailed explanation of the parameters' meanings and how to enable them using DSN_PROFILE_TABLE. This information is also documented in the *DB2 10 for z/OS Managing Performance* (SC19-2978) guide under the heading "Modeling a production environment on a test subsystem."

It is important to note, however, that a customer who copies statistics from a DB2 for z/OS Version 8 production environment to a non-production environment using DB2 10 for z/OS (or DB2 9 for z/OS) will not be able to reproduce the new CLUSTERRATIO formula without running DB2 9 for z/OS or DB2 10 for z/OS RUNSTATS on representative production data. However, copying DB2 9 for z/OS production statistics to a DB2 10 for z/OS pre-production environment will allow an accurate representation of what the statistics would be in DB2 10 for z/OS production, provided that RUNSTATS was run in DB2 9 for z/OS with system parameter STATCLUS set to ENHANCED (default) and the KEYCARD option was used.

Minimizing exposure to regression across REBIND

After arguing the case for REBIND in DB2 10 for z/OS Conversion Mode, it is important to revisit the reason why customers often avoid REBIND: the risk of query performance (access path) regression. Despite taking steps to ensure a stable statistics base is established, and potentially pre-production access path analysis performed, many customers may prefer to reduce the opportunity for any access path regression during migration. However, the non-access path reasons for REBIND make a compelling case to perform REBIND early in the DB2 10 for z/OS CM migration.

For customers migrating from DB2 9 for z/OS, there is a significant enhancement to access plan management in DB2 10 for z/OS that allows customers to REBIND and potentially reuse the prior access path. The reason it is mentioned that this option is available for customers upon migrations from DB2 9 for z/OS, but not from DB2 for z/OS Version 8, is because the reuse of the prior plan depends on the internal Explain Data Block that is saved internally in DB2 9 for z/OS and later releases.

To reiterate, a REBIND in DB2 10 for z/OS will generate new runtime structures, which means re-enablement of SPROCs and avoiding puffing and tolerance of the prior release runtime structures. It provides exploitation of DBM1 31-bit virtual storage constraint relief, new runtime optimizations, and safety from any quality issues with runtime structures from a prior release. Despite all those positives, there is a chance of an access path regression due to REBIND choosing a new access path. Let us not forget, however, that a new access path choice in the majority of cases provides similar or improved performance. But the reality is that many customers want to avoid that opportunity for regression.

The new BIND/REBIND parameter APREUSE will try to reuse the prior access path for each query in the package. The only value options for APREUSE are NO/NONE (the default), which means do not reuse the prior plan—consistent with standard BIND/REBIND behavior—or ERROR, which will try to reuse the prior plan but will fail the package BIND/REBIND if the prior plan cannot be reused.

For customers who want to obtain the new runtime structures, runtime optimizations, and virtual storage constraint, but without risking access path regression, REBIND with the APREUSE(ERROR) option is a good solution for migration from DB2 9 for z/OS to DB2 10 for z/OS. These customers can REBIND again later without APREUSE to explore optimizer improvements after their migration has stabilized.

Packages that fail to reuse the prior plan with APREUSE will remain as they were from the prior release, and customers must choose whether to REBIND to potentially obtain a new access path or leave these packages to be rebound at a later time.

Customers migrating from either DB2 for z/OS Version 8 or DB2 9 for z/OS to DB2 10 for z/OS will automatically be able to exploit the plan management fallback capability upon access path regression. The system parameter default in DB2 10 for z/OS is PLANMGMT=EXTENDED, which means that a REBIND will store the prior copy as the PREVIOUS, and an ORIGINAL will also be stored if one does not already exist. Upon experiencing a performance regression, customers may choose to REBIND SWITCH(PREVIOUS) or REBIND SWITCH(ORIGINAL) to restore a prior copy.

Switching back to a copy that was bound in a prior release means you are returning to the old runtime structure, which, as discussed, requires some additional CPU resource consumption to puff up the runtime structures to the format of the current release and also loses optimizations such as SPROCs.

Items Planned for Post-GA Delivery

The first items to mention here are APREUSE and APCOMPARE. These features are introduced with APAR PM25679. These options of BIND REPLACE and REBIND provide a way to generate a new SQL runtime but, at the same time, ask DB2 10 for z/OS to give you the old access path wherever possible. So, if you have previously rebound under DB2 9 for z/OS, this will mitigate the risk of access path change on the first BIND REPLACE or REBIND under DB2 10 for z/OS.

What to do if CPU performance regression occurs

When you encounter a possible CPU performance regression during migration to DB2 10 for z/OS, the first challenge is to verify that a CPU regression actually occurred and to properly qualify the problem to specific connection types, packages, and plans. To do so, you need to find valid comparison points in the real production environment pre- and post- the migration to DB2 10 for z/OS. The best approach is to factor out the batch processing because it can be highly variable based on the business operational calendar. You can then compare the performance data for the period on DB2 for z/OS Version 8 or DB2 9 for z/OS with the corresponding period under DB2 10 for z/OS. As a starting point, you can use a combination of statistics trace data, accounting trace data, and workload indicators to ensure you have valid comparison points and can identify the nature of the problem.

1. To determine whether a CPU regression occurred at migration, find an interval of several days with a comparable SQL profile across the DB2 for z/OS releases. For a valid comparison, you need a corresponding interval that has a similar number of total SQL requests and a similar distribution across the different types of SQL statements (SELECT, INSERT, UPDATE, DELETE, and so on). If you find that the SQL profile has changed significantly, the application workload has changed and a valid comparison for CPU regression is not possible.

2. Compare performance data for the identified period in the DB2 for z/OS Version 8 or DB2 9 for z/OS release with data from the corresponding period in the DB2 10 for z/OS release. You can use a combination of the statistics and accounting traces to check whether you have the same pattern across the DB2 releases.

   a. In the statistics trace data, start by comparing the CPU times for the following contexts:

   • Task control blocks (TCB) and service request blocks (SRB) for the MSTR address space.
   • Task control blocks (TCB), service request blocks (SRB), and specialty engine service request blocks for the DBM1 address space. The split between central processor and specialty engine time for the DBM1 address space is likely to be different between DB2 for z/OS Version 8 or DB2 9 for z/OS compared with DB2 10 for z/OS because CPU for prefetch and deferred write activity is now eligible for zIIP offload.

- Task control blocks (TCB) and service request blocks (SRB) for the IRLM address space.

b. In the accounting trace data, compare the Class 2 CPU times for each connection type, general purpose processors and for specialty engines, and check for the numbers of SQL requests, including the following workload indicators:

- The numbers of SQL statements for data manipulation, by type of statement (SELECT, INSERT, UPDATE, FETCH, and so on)
- The numbers of commit operations, rollback operations, getpage operations, and buffer pool updates
- The amount of read and write activity in terms of the number of I/O operations and the number of pages involved

c. Combine the statistics trace data and accounting trace data:

- Normalize the values by dividing the CPU time values by the number of commit and rollback operations. This assumes that the amount of batch activity factored out is relatively small. The resulting values are in terms of "CPU millisecond per commit or rollback."
- Stack the various components of CPU resource consumption. For example:

```
MSTR TCB CPU–time / (commits + rollbacks)
MSTR SRB CPU–time / (commits + rollbacks)
DBM1 TCB CPU–time / (commits + rollbacks)
DBM1 SRB CPU–time / (commits + rollbacks)
DBM1 IIP SRB CPU–time / (commits + rollbacks)
IRLM TCB CPU–time / (commits + rollbacks)
IRLM SRB CPU–time / (commits + rollbacks)
Average Class 2 CP CPU * occurrences / (commits + rollbacks)
Average Class 2 SE CPU * occurrences / (commits + rollbacks)
```

3. Compare the number of getpage operations for the corresponding intervals. If you find a significant increase in the numbers of getpage operations across releases (for comparable application workloads), access path changes are the most likely cause of the CPU regression.

Additional post-GA items

Additional items planned for post-GA delivery include the following:

- In DB2 10 for z/OS, you will be able to delete a data sharing member (APAR PM31009). Deleting a DB2 member will require a quiesce of the data sharing group.

- Inline LOBs will be introduced for SPT01 to gain the benefits of data compression and improve BIND/REBIND performance (APAR PM27811).
- Enhancements for new DBA authorities (APAR PM28296):

  ○ Prevent privileged users from stopping audit traces
  ○ No implicit system privileges for DBADM

- Online REORG concurrency for materializing deferred ALTERs (APAR PM25648).
- Temporal enhancements:

  ○ TIMESTAMP WITH TIMEZONE support (APAR PM31314)
  ○ Enhancement for data replication (APAR PM31315)
  ○ ALTER ADD COLUMN, propagate to history table (APAR PM31313)

- New system profile filters based on "client info" fields (APAR PM28500):

  ○ Three new columns for user ID, application name, and workstation.
  ○ Wildcard support: If column is '*' then all threads pass that qualification.

- A new DB2 system parameter to force deletion of coupling facility (CF) structures on group restart (APAR PM28925). This feature is aimed at disaster recovery. We want to avoid a situation during a disaster restart of using "stale" information in the CF structures. When the DB2 member starts and it is the first member to connect to the structure, it wipes out those structures and forces a group restart.
- Relief for the incompatible change in the behavior of the CHAR() function when applied to decimal data by using APAR PM29124 to restore the previous behavior that existed prior to DB2 10 for z/OS.
- Real storage monitoring enhancements (APAR PM24723); this APAR also provides protection for overcommitment of available real storage.
- Hash LOAD performance (APAR PM31214).
- DSSIZE greater than 64 GB (APAR yet to be announced).

Note

---

z/OS Real Storage Manager (RSM) APAR OA35885 is a prerequisite to the enhanced storage monitoring capability provided by DB2 APAR PM24723. DB2 APAR PM24723 is strongly recommended for production use of DB2 10 for z/OS.

   We strongly advise customers *not* to go into a major production environment *without* the proper monitoring of real and auxiliary storage usage as provided by this APAR and DB2 APAR PM24723. Together, these two APARs provide DB2 10 for z/OS with statistics on real and auxiliary storage use in relation to the 64-bit memory objects allocated by DB2 for z/OS above the 2 GB bar.

DB2 10 for z/OS can request z/OS to provide information about real and auxiliary storage based on a particular addressing range. This functionality enables proper monitoring when you have multiple DB2 subsystems running on the same LPAR. It also provides some protection against system paging, overcommitting real storage, or running out of auxiliary storage. DB2 can free unused memory back to the z/OS operating system.

When Should You Migrate to DB2 10 for z/OS?

A "normal" migration is moving one version at a time every three years. For customers with even earlier versions, the ability to skip a migration cycle will be attractive, but this ability is not "something for nothing." Customers need to consider the tradeoffs and challenges in a "skip version" migration. Most customers who migrate to a new version some three years after the general announcement (GA) of the respective new release are already on DB2 9 for z/OS.

The project for skipping a release is larger. While the testing and rollout are only a little greater than a single-version migration, the education and remediation work is roughly double the size; most project plans estimate 150 percent. Consider the timing carefully. Improvements in DB2 9 for z/OS are delayed with a "skip" release migration plan. You may need to apply for extended service on DB2 for z/OS Version 8.

In summary:

- We recommend the regular application of preventive service maintenance. It should be a continual process.
- Testing should be performed over and above that performed by DB2 for z/OS Development.
- CST testing still does *not* replace the need for customer regression/stress testing to certify production readiness in a specific customer installation of a new DB2 release.
- You must be prepared to tolerate some "bumps in the road."
- Customers who are not prepared to take risk-mitigating actions and have no tolerance for "bumps in the road" should not be early adopters and should migrate directly to DB2 9 for z/OS.

For customers who are still running DB2 for OS/390 Version 7, the option to skip from DB2 for z/OS Version 8 to DB2 10 for z/OS is very attractive and makes the current path clear. Customers who have just migrated to DB2 for z/OS Version 8 may like this alternative, for the short term. DB2 10 for z/OS supports migration from DB2 9 for z/OS NFM or from DB2 for z/OS Version 8 NFM. Customers not yet running DB2 for z/OS Version 8 or DB2 9 for z/OS should plan to migrate first to DB2 for z/OS Version 8, as preparation for an eventual migration to DB2 10 for z/OS.

We estimate that about one in every five customers migrated using a "skip version" technique from DB2 for OS/390 Version 5 to DB2 for OS/390 Version 7, and we expect to see a similar proportion this time with DB2 10 for z/OS. The savings for skipping a version migration are less than 50 percent, since the education and needed application and administration changes are about the same. Customers who do choose a skip migration report that the project takes longer—about 50 percent longer than a normal migration path.

Changing from DB2 for z/OS Version 8 or an earlier release to DB2 10 for z/OS will require a cultural shift that some describe as "culture shock." If customers spend the bulk of their migration project time in testing, savings could be up to 40 percent. But most customer plans should expect a 20 to 25 percent reduction, compared with having to execute two release migrations.

The tradeoff for skipping is primarily the later delivery of DB2 9 for z/OS improvements, namely CPU savings (especially in utilities and disk savings via index compression), improved insert and update throughput rates, improved SQL, and pureXML for developer productivity, as well as better availability.

Summary

To summarize, DB2 10 for z/OS is a very good release in terms of the opportunities for price/performance and scalability improvements. There is significant DBM1 31-bit virtual storage constraint relief (VSCR) to be gained after the rebind of static SQL plans and packages soon after reaching DB2 10 for z/OS Conversion Mode (CM). You can exploit the 1 MB size real storage page frames on z10 and z196 processors, provided the DB2 local buffer pools are long-term page fixed. There are also improvements in terms of reduced latch contention and latch management overhead.

Over and above the "out-of-the-box" performance improvements as a result of BIND/ REBIND of static SQL plans/packages and the use of 1 MB size real storage page frames, DB2 10 for z/OS offers opportunities for further price/performance improvements *provided you have enough real storage provisioned on the LPAR*. It is a classic tradeoff between increased real storage provision in order to reduce CPU resource consumption. This includes making more use of persistent threads both for legacy CICS and IMS/TM applications as well as the use of high-performance DBATs for DDF transactional workloads.

If you have enough real storage provisioned on the LPAR, you can make greater use of packages bound with the BIND option RELEASE(DEALLOCATE) with these persistent threads. But you must recognize that the increased use of RELEASE(DEALLOCATE) is a tradeoff; it will lead to increased storage consumption, and you will need to plan for additional real storage resource consumption over and above the required 10 percent to 30 percent increase just to stand still when migrating to DB2 10 for z/OS.

The use of packages bound with the BIND option RELEASE(DEALLOCATE) with persistent threads can also reduce concurrency because BIND/REBIND and SQL DDL activity will not be able to break into work.

DB2 10 for z/OS also provides an opportunity for the greatly enhanced vertical scalability of an individual DB2 member in data sharing and the potential for DB2 consolidation and possibly LPAR consolidation.

You must carefully plan, provision, and monitor real storage resource consumption. Early customer adopters of DB2 10 for z/OS, migrating from either DB2 for z/OS Version 8 or DB2 9 for z/OS, should make plans and take extra care to mitigate the risk of instability. Those steps include:

✓ Plan regular full "major" maintenance drops within a continuous process.
✓ Use CST/RSU recommended maintenance and exploit Enhanced HOLDDATA.
✓ Perform application regression and stress testing to keep problems away from production.
✓ Be prepared to tolerate some "bumps in the road."

Case Study:
Kela Invests in Improving
Service Delivery for Finland's Citizens

Capitalizing on new functionality
to gain efficiencies and simplify IT management

"By improving the performance and efficiency of the Kela database processing capabilities, we're now better able to meet the growing demand for social services among our main constituency, the citizens of Finland."

—Jarmo Männikkö, Database Senior System Programmer, Kela

Based in Helsinki, Finland, and employing about 6,000 people, Kela is Finland's primary social insurance institution. Its wide portfolio of benefits covers everything from pensions, disability, health insurance, and rehabilitation to unemployment insurance, small-child care and family allowances, maternity grants, student benefits, general housing allowances, conscripts' allowances, and special assistance for immigrants. In 2011, Kela delivered benefits valued at roughly EUR12.6 billion to about four million applicants. In an average year, the agency generates approximately 11 million points of contact with Finnish citizens through its online, phone-based, and physical channels.

Challenge

Like most social service agencies, Kela faces the constant challenge of providing high levels of service to its constituents in a constrained resource environment. As Kela turned increasingly toward the online delivery of information and services, and customer quality expectations have continually risen, the agency recognized the need to steadily invest in improving the performance and efficiency of its service delivery infrastructure. An example of this commitment was its 2011 decision to upgrade the two IBM® System z® mainframes at the core of its infrastructure to a pair of IBM zEnterprise™ 196 mainframes running the IBM z/OS environment.

To complement its investment while further improving its systems' performance and cost-effectiveness, Kela sought to upgrade its database processing capabilities. The agency's specific goals were to reduce overall CPU usage, improve response time, and reduce storage requirements, which together would help the company more effectively execute its mission of serving citizens.

Solution

It had been a decade since the agency first selected IBM DB2 software, on the strength of its security, to store highly sensitive information, and Kela was a satisfied client. Kela saw the opportunity to build on its success by upgrading its database platform to an IBM

DB2 10 for z/OS solution. The upgrade project, executed almost entirely by Kela personnel, required just three months from installation to production. Kela uses the enhanced DB2 solution to support its existing distributed IBM WebSphere® Application Server software environments, which represent roughly one million daily transactions, as well as IBM CICS Transaction Server software and batch-processing workloads, representing about nine million daily transactions.

As Kela continues to expand its base of distributed applications, it also wanted to gain a better understanding of how different segments of the transaction affected response time. This required the ability to monitor transactions from the customer level to the DB2 processing. To achieve this, Kela implemented the IBM Tivoli® OMEGAMON® XE for DB2 Performance Expert on z/OS tool. By using the Extended Insight Dashboard feature, Kela monitored how much of the overall processing time and workload were spent at the customer, network, and database processing portions of the transaction. That visibility gave it the inside information it needed to optimize the execution parameters of different kinds of transactions.

Benefits

- Lowers CPU requirements by up to 15 percent, resulting in lower overall software costs
- Reduces storage consumption and associated hardware and software costs
- Enables Kela to develop new services faster because of enhanced support for XML functionality
- Increases IT staff productivity through automated tuning functionality

Case Study:
Primerica Improves Efficiency
and Gains More Flexibility

Capitalizing on the latest improvements
in IBM DB2 for z/OS technology

"DB2 provides us with a foundation such that two and three years down the road, we know we won't be impeded in developing new applications with our partners or in rolling out new smartphone apps to our agents."

—Bill Raser, Senior Vice President of Data Administration
and Mainframe Systems Support, Primerica

Headquartered in Duluth, Georgia, Primerica is the largest independent financial services marketing company in North America, with offerings that include term life insurance, mutual funds, variable annuities, and loans. Through a network of some 90,000 licensed sales representatives, the company focuses on the middle income market segment. In addition to an insured base of more than 4.3 million lives, Primerica has approximately two million customers who maintain investment accounts with the company.

A Strategic Readiness for Innovation

The insurance business is by its very nature focused on being ready for the unexpected, for being prudently prepared for what comes down the road. To Primerica chief information officer (CIO) David Wade, that philosophy is also embodied in the company's strategic technology planning approach. "We've long believed that staying current with our software is strategically important for us," says Wade. "We never want to be in a position where some potentially game-changing technology becomes available and we'd have to tell our CEO, 'Sorry, but we're not going to be able to embrace it because we haven't kept up with our core technology upgrades.' To us, leadership means capitalizing on the latest advances."

One important measure of that dedication is the company's longtime commitment to the IBM System z as its most strategic technology asset. When Primerica decided in 2011 to upgrade to the powerful new IBM zEnterprise® 196 (z196) server, it marked a 30-year relationship with IBM. Its commitment to investing in foundational technology is also seen on the software side in its decision to upgrade to an IBM DB2 10 for z/OS data server. As with the IBM System z, DB2 data servers support the company's hundreds of core business applications, from internal processing to the many applications accessed through the web, allowing thousands of Primerica agents to take an application from a laptop, PC, mobile digital device, or any device that supports traditional HTML web standards.

Making the Case for Change

Taking advantage of the latest technology advancements in DB2 10 was essential for helping Primerica remain competitive, and speed was a crucial factor. For customers and agents, the prevailing expectation for processing new applications, once a matter of days or weeks, is now measured in minutes. For Primerica, which takes in some 80 percent of its new business electronically, that translates into faster and more efficient processing from start to finish.

The ever-changing dynamics of the insurance marketplace also put a premium on flexibility. Customer and agent needs for new products and applications are always evolving, as is the need for Primerica to share data and collaborate with third parties in the insurance ecosystem. That means the more nimble Primerica can be in developing new applications and linking with partners, the better it can compete.

Mitigating Risk with Flexible Upgrade Options

These business rationales underpinned the decision to upgrade the company's DB2 data server to Version 10. Relying on a small team of database administrators and System z programmers, Primerica completed the first phase of its upgrade, to conversion mode, in approximately five months, the majority of which was spent in testing. Bill Raser, senior vice president of data administration and System z support at Primerica and a leader of the project, points to the flexible upgrade options of DB2 10 for z/OS as a key reason for the project's success. "The fact that we could upgrade first in conversion mode and then step up to new function mode made our process very reliable and seamless," Raser explains. "It gave us a high degree of confidence that our core business applications wouldn't be disrupted."

The Path to Greater Efficiency

At this point in the project, Raser points to an improvement in workload performance as the most direct benefit of the upgrade. "Our overall impression is that we have already seen a roughly 6 percent performance increase by taking advantage of support for large [1 MB] pages in DB2 Version 10," says Raser. "Later on, we project CPU savings of as much as 10 percent for some applications."

Raser believes that the next phase of the project, deploying the DB2 10 for z/OS data server in new function mode (NFM), will unleash a series of additional benefits, including faster and more flexible application development capabilities made possible by stronger Extensible Markup Language (XML) support."

A big part of rolling out new applications is our ability to share data and processes with business partners," says Raser. "By giving us stronger pureXML capabilities, we are better able to communicate and interact with our partners using web technology and thus are more flexible in rolling out advanced new applications that ultimately enable us to serve the customer better." And the big picture? "DB2 provides us with a foundation such that two and three years down the road, we know we won't be impeded in developing new applications with our partners or in rolling out new smartphone apps to our agents. We also believe that by exploiting temporal technology, we'll be able to generate further application development cost savings in the future."

Case Study:
GAD Upgrades Database Systems
to Boost Power and Productivity

IT staff migrates to IBM DB2 10 and IBM IMS 12
software to modernize its banking infrastructure

"We quickly realized that DB2 10 could accommodate our annual 5 to 10 percent increase in transaction volume without forcing us to increase CPU capacity, which represents an important cost savings."

—Andreas Wagner, First Line Manager, GAD

GAD eG (GAD) is the data processing center and IT service provider for a variety of co-operative banks known as *Volksbanken* and *Raiffeisenbanken,* as well as a software development company for the cooperative organization *Genossenschaftlicher FinanzVerbund* in north and central Germany. Its responsibilities range from development and sales of banking software to provisioning of electronic banking services to IT consulting and education. GAD has approximately 1,800 employees who serve 460 branch banks, support 29.6 million customer accounts, and oversee more than 70,000 distributed devices.

As the only provider serving corporation banks in northern and central Germany, GAD has seen its revenue increase from EUR620 million in 2009 to EUR650 million in 2010. However, hosting all data, transactions, and information for high-volume banking establishments on its mainframe means that GAD is always looking for ways to reduce costs, as well as satisfy strict government audit requirements, by continuously modernizing its mission-critical IT infrastructure.

The challenge for GAD's data processing center is remaining resilient to meet business mandates from the banks, as well as round-the-clock access for online customers. In fact, nothing less than 24x7 availability for its center's many applications and roughly 170 systems is acceptable, as GAD routinely processes as many as 400 to 600 transactions per second during peak throughput periods. This transaction volume, which adds up to a staggering 13.3 billion transactions per year, continues to increase by 5 to 10 percent annually. In an environment characterized by ever-increasing workloads, identifying new ways to reduce application downtime remains an ongoing priority.

To provision vital applications and support its banking customers online, GAD operates a total infrastructure solution called bank21, which integrates diverse platforms, applications, and technologies to deliver maximum customer value. In the course of conducting IBM IMS™ 12 Quality Program Plan (QPP) testing, GAD quickly identified the potential for new, productivity-enhancing features and improved CPU utilization that could be realized by upgrading its IBM DB2 data server environment to IBM DB2 10 for z/OS for transaction processing.

Upgrading to DB2 10 Delivers Out-of-the-Box Stability

GAD upgraded to IBM DB2 10 for z/OS and began by cloning its production environment within the test environment to run massive batch programs. "The first thing we wanted was out-of-the-box stability and resilience from DB2 10—support from IBM made that happen, eliminating potential compatibility issues with our legacy systems," says Andreas Wagner, first line manager at GAD. "Ultimately, we were able to run 'big batch' processing in the new version of DB2 without any application changes, which saved us a lot of time and effort."

Saving time and effort is important, as GAD operates many four-way and eight-way data sharing systems, with workloads running through IMS and transactions through DB2. "Besides production workload, 500 developers are also using DB2, so it's a big part in our environment," says Wagner.

Serving GAD customers requires a large and complex production environment. Of the company's 45 data sharing systems, fully two-thirds of these systems are dedicated solely to provisioning services for its different production environments. These environments are split into different logical partitions (LPARs) with different numbers of data sharing members per LPAR, depending on the workload by GAD's customers.

Realizing infrastructure improvements and savings across such complex IT infrastructure required a new approach that only DB2 10 for z/OS could provide. "We began testing the new features in DB2 10 at a granular level to see where we could improve performance and efficiency," says Wagner. "In the process, we were able to get better visibility into CPU usage and gain functionality we never had before."

For example, leveraging the new functionality in DB2 10 allowed GAD to perform and monitor parallel binds for the first time. Parallel binding in DB2 10 enables GAD to optimize tasks to achieve minimum elapsed time for bind processing during new or changed application rollout. "Being able to control parallel tasks at bind time is an important feature that significantly reduces downtime during our application rollouts," says Wagner. "It gives us more throughput for the binding process."

Standardizing on System z Speeds Performance, Maintenance, and Scalability

Considering the many critical-path databases, production systems, and LPARs that make up GAD's bank21 solution, it's not difficult to imagine that the underlying hardware would also need to conform to the highest possible standards of security, performance, and reliability to meet the company's needs—and IBM System z delivered. "We're now running eight z196 servers with z Integrated Information Processor (zIIP) coupling, and that gives us a real edge for simplifying maintenance and rolling out fixes," says Wagner. "In a distributed environment, depending on the number of affected systems, database maintenance tasks can take weeks—System z allows us to maintain 170 systems in a fraction of the time."

Further advantages GAD experienced with z196 servers were faster CPUs and the ability to add more CPUs and memory on the fly, making it easier to support the company's 45 data sharing groups. The hardware also provides essential performance and scalability to support GAD's bank21 solution, which utilizes IBM WebSphere software for both its web and application servers. To facilitate integration between the DB2 for z/OS data server and the OO-Java–based bank21 application portion, the company selected IBM WebSphere Application Server. With the new option from DB2 10 for z/OS, the customer expects opportunities for optimized price performance (e.g., using high-performance database access threads).

Reducing CPU Usage Helps Keep Costs Flat as Business Grows

DB2 10 provided improved visibility across GAD's vast assortment of existing databases, along with startling new insights into CPU usage. "We quickly realized that DB2 10 could accommodate our annual 5-to-10 percent increase in transaction volume without forcing us to increase CPU capacity, which represents an important cost savings," says Wagner. "We were pleasantly surprised by DB2 10's ability to reduce CPU usage with better memory access and shorter processor times, because that puts us in a great position to handle even greater increases in transaction volume moving forward."

Adopting Parallel Binds Provides Time Savings of 50 Percent

By taking advantage of the features in DB2 10 new function mode, GAD was also able to accelerate its twice-yearly application rollouts by taking a new approach to the bind/rebind process for loading and unloading data. "DB2 10 enabled us to cut the time to do parallel binds by 50 percent during QPP testing, which helps us maintain 24x7 availability," says Wagner. "We saw improved availability and performance for loading and unloading data in our production system too. With the capability of DB2 10 to provide optimized parallel bind for static BINDs, the time required for application roll-out bind processing at GAD could be reduced by over 50 percent."

Accelerated Application Provisioning Boosts Productivity

Among the software's many time-saving new features, DB2 10 also adds more support for DBA tasks by online schema evolution, which makes it possible to change indexes and table spaces without having to unload the data or drop and re-create the objects. "Features like online schemas and DB2 10 compilers gave us some rapid productivity gains for provisioning applications, so that we can service the environment and deal with increased workloads without adding additional staff," says Wagner.

In addition, new audit functionality in DB2 10 greatly simplifies the process of meeting government requirements, an important issue in the banking industry. "We have activated the audit feature on all tables on the mainframe to run special traces," says Wagner. "So we now have greater security and peace of mind for legal compliance and reporting tasks."

Engaging with IBM Positions GAD to Meet Future Business Needs

As GAD has been using IMS databases for back-end workloads through its bank21 solution, participating in the IMS 12 Quality Partnership Program gave the company an opportunity to work with the latest version of IMS ahead of its formal GA launch. "We rolled out IMS 12 in our production environment before it reached GA, and there are some interesting features which we also plan to activate in the near future," says Wagner. "Because we've had such a long relationship with IBM, we know we can rely on them to give us innovative solutions. The best part is knowing that expert service and support is always there whenever our evolving business needs demand it."

Case Study:
DB2 10 for z/OS Eases Workload
Consolidation for Bankdata and JN Data

New features and a smooth upgrade process
ease workload consolidation project

"DB2 10 came at a very good time for us, as it will allow us to better cope with the very large increase in volumes we're about to experience."

—Frank Petersen, Systems Programmer, JN Data

Bankdata exists to provide high-quality financial IT solutions to the 15 Danish banks that are its customers, and it is the largest IT developer in southern Denmark. JN Data specializes in the provision of IT operations and engineering for large Danish financial institutions, including Jyske Bank, Nykredit, BEC, and SDC. In 2010, JN Data acquired the IT operations unit of Bankdata, making it responsible for the combined workloads of both sets of customers.

During the past two years, both organizations have been working hard to integrate their IT processes and procedures, with the main DB2 workloads due to be consolidated in October 2012. Undertaking a major DB2 version upgrade during such a critical time may seem strange at first, but according to Systems Programmer Frank Petersen, "DB2 10 came at a very good time for us, as it will allow us to better cope with the very large increase in volumes we're about to experience."

The workload consolidation will effectively double the Bankdata transaction and data volumes supported by JN Data, but the considerable virtual storage constraint relief (VSCR) enhancements delivered by DB2 10 for z/OS will allow the additional workload to be accommodated without having to increase the number of DB2 subsystems within the production data sharing groups. "The enhanced online schema change capabilities also made it easier for us to implement the physical design changes required by the merger, while minimizing the availability impact to our production workload," added Frank.

As Bankdata had been an active member of the DB2 10 beta program, key technical staff were able to explore its new features and build their technical knowledge and confidence in the new release at an early stage. That experience allowed them to begin the DB2 10 implementation project very soon after the product became generally available in October 2010, with the last of the production DB2 systems successfully entering New Function Mode in the spring of 2012. "Overall the upgrade process has been a smooth one. We were especially pleased with the increased concurrency during the DB2 catalog restructuring, which reduced the impact to our production workload compared to previous upgrades," said Frank.

What other benefits has Frank observed as a result of the upgrade to DB2 10? "We have seen a few CPU reductions, but this has not been such a major benefit for us as our workload is mainly composed of very well-tuned static SQL—we don't have much distributed or dynamic SQL," he said. "However, the new statement-level accounting data is a great new feature, and we have already expanded our performance data warehouse to collect and exploit this valuable new feature."

JN Data currently has just two temporal tables in production as most developers have been very busy with the merger, but Frank sees considerable potential in the new feature. "The up-front productivity benefits are very welcome, of course, but reducing complexity and making future maintenance easier are just as important to us," he noted.

IT infrastructure upgrades often struggle to demonstrate direct business benefits, but in a period of considerable change and technical challenge for JN Data and Bankdata, the new features in DB2 10 for z/OS have made a timely and valuable contribution to the overall success of the workload integration project.

Case Study:
Bank Hapoalim Improves Efficiency,
Reduces Tape Usage by 25 Percent

Bank views IBM DB2 for z/OS software upgrade as key to delivering innovative banking solutions

"DB2 10's back-out capability allows us to take some of our routine processes, which used to require a time-consuming forward recovery, and just back out changes instead, so we're saving time and improving availability."

—Michael Shaul, database administration team leader, Bank Hapoalim

Founded in 1921, Bank Hapoalim is Israel's leading financial services group and one of its largest banks. It services corporate and retail customers and has a significant international presence, with branches, subsidiaries, and representative offices in North America, Latin America, Europe, East Asia, Turkey, and Australia.

Challenge

Bank Hapoalim prides itself on an innovative approach to banking, and the performance of its underlying IT infrastructure is critical to delivering on that strategy. Keeping pace with the bank's ongoing and accelerating drive for business innovation requires a continuous focus on optimizing workload, memory, and storage management. It also means ensuring that the bank's database management system provides the necessary scalability, reliability, and security.

The linchpin of this drive for continuous improvement is the bank's IBM DB2 for z/OS data server software, which it upgrades with every new version. During the execution of its latest upgrade to IBM DB2 10 for z/OS data server software, the bank needed to minimize business interruptions.

Solution

Bank Hapoalim is a longtime DB2 for z/OS data server software user, having adopted the technology in the 1980s. Since then, it has been on the forefront of exploiting the new functionality offered in each subsequent release.

"We began planning for our DB2 9 to DB2 10 upgrade project very shortly after the new release went into general availability," says Michael Shaul, database administration team leader for Bank Hapoalim. "The actual upgrade process went very smoothly; I would say it was our easiest yet."

Easing the process was the DB2 for z/OS solution's highly scalable data-sharing environment, which makes the already highly available IBM mainframe running the z/OS operating system even more available by clustering it in a shared-disk configuration. For the first time, Bank Hapoalim was able to keep part of its DB2 data server software workload active during the upgrade, minimizing the impact on the work. "We were able to upgrade one member at a time and keep our online workload running throughout the process with minimal disruption," says Michael.

Many businesses can make a strong case for a DB2 10 for z/OS data server software upgrade solely because of the potential CPU savings. Workloads at Bank Hapoalim, however, are predominantly COBOL using highly optimized and strictly controlled static SQL, so Michael was not expecting significant reductions. Nonetheless, the bank measured a CPU savings of around 3 percent in some batch workloads, while using 1 MB page frames.

The impact on tape usage, however, has been considerable. With the DB2 10 for z/OS data server software upgrade, system management facilities volumes are down by around 75 percent, which translates to an approximate 25 percent tape usage savings. In addition, according to Michael, DB2 10 for z/OS data server software contributes to process optimization. "DB2 10's back-out capability allows us to take some of our routine processes, which used to require a time-consuming forward recovery, and just back out changes instead, so we're saving time and improving availability."

True to history, Michael points to one more benefit of his company's upgrade to DB2 10 for z/OS data server software. "It's a prerequisite for the next release of DB2, and we're already looking forward to some of the new features and functions that are likely to be delivered."

Benefits

- Lowers system management facilities volumes by approximately 75 percent
- Reduces tape usage by around 25 percent
- Decreases CPU requirements for some batch workloads